MW00945664

Dr. Golden

Please enjoy my Mothers

Deborah [illegible]

11/1/24

SELF-MOTHERING

MY MOTHERS' COUNCIL

DEBORAH L. BERNAL M.D.

A DIVISION OF HAY HOUSE

Chicago Manual Style

Balboa Press books may be ordered through booksellers or by contacting:

Balboa Press
A Division of Hay House
1663 Liberty Drive
Bloomington, IN 47403
www.balboapress.com
1 (877) 407-4847

Print information available on the last page.

ISBN: 978-1-5043-8167-3 (sc)
ISBN: 978-1-5043-8168-0 (hc)
ISBN: 978-1-5043-8222-9 (e)

Library of Congress Control Number: 2017909073

Balboa Press rev. date: 07/07/2017

Contents

ACKNOWLEDGMENTS

I WOULD LIKE TO THANK my mother for bringing me into this incarnation and my mother's mothers before her and all of my ancestors on whose shoulders I stand. The lineage that motivated and nurtured us into existence is all part of the history that has made my mother who she is and me who I am.

Thank you to my children, who have given me the opportunity to experience the wonder of motherhood and have allowed me to grow up with them in this journey we call life. The journey continues as we all continue our evolution together.

Thank you to all the mothers in my Mothers' Council. Thank you for the counsel you have given me through your life's journey and in my life directly.

Thank you to my sacred partners who have been with me on the journey of motherhood, aunties, grandmothers, godmothers, mentors, role models, sisters, and sister friends who are with me still or have transitioned along the way. May we support each other with love and forgiveness! May we live a life free of regret, embracing our lessons and moving forward with passion and conviction, always reaching back to bring others along!

Prologue

I view every appointment in my doctor's office as a sacred appointment during this point in my medical practice. The word *practice* is appropriate because it never seems to be routine. It is always as much a learning experience for me as for my patients. I see myself first and foremost as a storyteller. I want to listen with compassion to a patient's story to find out what we know up until now. The story is the beginning. The mystery unfolds. Questions and curiosity bring about more revelations to me and often to the patients themselves as they share, hearing themselves answer the questions. They often speak their secrets, sometimes for the first time out loud. Some unanswered questions require investigation, such as diagnostic testing or imaging, but there are other open-ended questions as well, such as, "What are *you* willing to do to change the direction of *your* life?" I asked myself, "What can I share to inspire change without overwhelming them or causing despair and hopelessness? What does the spirit of their ancestors and spirit guides want me to tell them that I can hear and share with these patients that they have been denying in their lives?"

So it occurred one day with a patient—a postmenopausal woman about my age, prior to retirement, mothering other adults but with no biological children of her own. She was an overcommitted woman without appropriate boundaries, a martyr of sorts, who wanted to be an equal fifty/fifty to her male counterpart. Therefore, she wanted to do her "fair share" especially with the physical labor! She did her half to the detriment of her physical health. She was knowledgeable and body aware of what she was doing as she was doing it. She knew it was a problem, but like most people in denial of the full ramifications of their behavior, the full consequences came the next day, like being hit by a Mack truck. The Superwoman symbol on her chest had tire tracks running through it. She was going through unnecessary suffering. To inspire her to hang up the Superwoman outfit for good, I asked, "If you were taking care of the little girl inside you, what would have been different?" I was asking her to do Self-Mothering. I needed her to look at herself as a precious child that needs to be guided and protected and not allowed to come to harm. I needed her to be the mother of that child, once harmed, who would nurture and heal the wounds with love, compassion, understanding, and wisdom.

This little book, *Self-Mothering*, was created to answer the question for her and all the other superwomen and supermoms like her I see in my practice, in my life, as well as that woman in the mirror—myself. I needed to define what self-mothering looks like and how it can work in one's life. How can I expand this concept to make it feel real and doable? The lessons I share with my patients are never just for my patients alone; they are always lessons for patients to come and myself as well. We are all connected. It is a sacred contract.

Chapter 1

My Mothers' Council

No one person can be the end all and be all for anyone. The ancient African proverb, "It takes a village to raise a child" plays out in our adult life as "It takes a council to raise an adult." We never stop changing, but are we growing? Are we conscious of choices we make in our development as human beings, pushing humanity forward? If you are asking yourself these questions, I am sharing my journey so far with you. Just as roads have been built and buildings and civilizations have come and gone, our human thoughts are being created and remodeled regularly. I choose to make this an active process. I know my life has been preceded by seekers who can lead and guide me. I realize I need mentors and role models all along the way and have been fortunate to have access to their wisdom.

Life can happen to us, or we can happen to life. Be responsible. Choose to be the captain of your ship rather than a martyr or a victim. Don't blame or complain. As Mahatma Gandhi said, "Be the change you want to see in the world." My mothers are helping me make those changes.

This book was on Post-it notes around the edges of my mirror in ideas and phrases gathered from the counsel of the mothers I gathered over the years. My council of mothers is gathered in my photo albums, my ancestral tributes, my library bookshelves, my dream journals, my cell phone notes and pictures, and the obituaries from a box on my altar. Every appointment is a divine appointment—a holy relationship. As an old English proverb states, "An idle mind is the devil's workshop." A fertile mind is the womb of creation. Ideas are conceived in the dark recesses of the mind. They are birthed through manifestation in real time in real-life, mundane daily circumstances that can illuminate us or keep us stuck going round and round but nowhere fast.

The Mothers' Council I have assembled in this book are some women I've chosen to counsel me in specific areas of their expertise and experience where I have questions. We need help from outside ourselves to see ourselves and to gauge our development. I was introduced to many of my mothers in childhood, figuratively, through books, stories, and history. I draw meaning from their words and lives. These are my role models. Those I do know personally I've come to know throughout my life, and I have drawn them from my personal reflection and connection. These are my board members. When I am deciding on an intention or trying to solve a problem I'm facing, I have a board of directors to consult. I reflect on their qualities to decide—who are the mothers I need for this situation, and why do I need them?

I have chosen to share mothers through the journeys of my many age-set transitions. I want to introduce all eleven categories of my mothers with a brief description of their qualities and how they have been helpful in the variety of difficulties. This information will be detailed in further chapters with specific examples from my Mothers' Council, one historical and the other personal for each of the maternal categories: Earth Mother, Doctor Mom, Mother Sister, Mother Wit, Lawyer Mother, Mentor Mother, Sexy Mama, Warrior Mother, Grandmother Mother, Queen Mother, and Godmother Mother.

Earth Mother

Our life cycle starts with our Earth Mother housing us on her interplanetary journey as she voyages through the cosmos. Our birth from our biological mother creates the material form of our existence from egg to embryo to infant. We need to feel our mother's love and know that we are worthy. We are children of God—innocent, guiltless, sinless, and pure. If we haven't gotten this feeling or knowledge from our upbringing, it is still our birthright. We must seek outside of ourselves to find this from our Earth Mother.

An Earth Mother's love is like Mother Nature. She is fertile, abundant, resourceful, and able to supply all our needs. She carries us in her womb, the sacred womb of creation. She feeds us from her bosom. She shares her life force. She guides our growth and development. She is the cradle of civilization. She delivers us into the world fully equipped. With this love, the world is our oyster.

I could find no better historical earth mother than Mother Earth herself. Nature has so much innate wisdom to share, and she is always available to us to experience her intelligence. She brings the laws of the universe and the laws of nature right to our doorstep. My earth mother mentor is Sabrina Johnson, a sister friend I became an instant friend with over twenty years ago. She has been my living mentor and role model for living close to nature and expressing the fullness of life.

Doctor Mom

Life happens. We experience the bumps and bruises of exploring our wonderful world. As toddlers we are watched and protected in our discovering creation; inadvertently, we get hurt, reinforcing the universal laws life teaches. For these mishaps we have Doctor Mom, who takes care of us when we are sick or injured. She bathes and bandages our wounds with her unconditional love. She takes care of us and assures us that everything will be all right. She curls up with us in bed to ease our suffering, allowing us to rest in her secure embrace. She heals and protects. With her love, we expect healing. We understand the lesson as part of our growth.

Doctor Mom embodies lifelong learning. Doctors are never finished learning their profession. They expect to practice the art of healing while not knowing everything—far from that! But they understand that the discovery is part of the process of healing, and healing is a divine right inherent to our being. We are travelers on this journey of life, here to discover meaning. Doctor Mom is our comforter, optimist, and guide. She is helping us heal ourselves through her own healing journey.

My historical Doctor Mom was an inspiration from my childhood when I heard of her and her work during a second collection at my Catholic church for her mission in India. This mother was not a doctor but dedicated her life to her healing work. Mother Teresa was an inspiration to me growing up. I was called from an early age to the medical profession as an avenue for my healing work. My Doctor Mom personal mentor has a life mission to heal the world, and she is not a doctor either. She is my aunt Pearlie, 96-years young and even younger at heart. She is the role model for self-healing and sharing her healing gifts with the world.

Mother Sister

Mother Sister is our childhood mother who plays and enjoys life but is like a big sister and keeps us in line. Our Mother Sister provides an ear to listen. She is available to give a helping hand. There is always a pat on the back to encourage us. She congratulates us with applause. She is always glad to see us. She is always prepared for a spontaneous pampering or help with a past-due project. She wants the very best of everything for us. She is by our side, hugging, pampering, reassuring, and playing—or behind the scenes, praying, visualizing, and surrendering to the divine.

She remains carefree by appreciating her work as play. She is never careless. She wants us to enjoy ourselves; however, she keeps our feet to the fire and makes us responsible. She understands that we teach others how to treat us. She knows how to set firm boundaries with love. She appreciates a job well done and relishes relaxing in life's pleasures.

I was captivated by the story of Helen Keller as a young child, but I was more curious about the teacher than the student. My research into the life of her teacher, Anne Sullivan, revealed her as Mother Sister of Helen Keller. She needed to break through the physical barriers of deafness and blindness as well as the emotional barriers of manipulation of this spoiled child in a dysfunctional family. My oldest sister, Yvonne, is my Mother Sister, who continues to be both playmate and groundbreaker for my path ahead.

Mother Wit

Mother Wit challenges us and keeps us on our toes. She is quick. She is sharp. She can always flip the script on us and keep us guessing. She is tricky and plays the devil's advocate. She shows us the loopholes. She is the temptress. She knows how to get under our skin and on our last nerve. She keeps us off guard and shows us our lessons. She does everything in our best interest. There is no meanness or spite, just honesty and truth. Her purpose is discovery. Her job is illumination. She is here to shake things up and challenge the status quo. She keeps us humble, loving, and forgiving.

When we were teenagers and our mothers couldn't tell us anything, it was a word to the wise from this mother that stopped us dead in our tracks. Without this blunt wisdom, we could find ourselves down a long and dangerous path far from the road we thought we were embarking upon. We need this mother at the crossroads of our decision making to bring to light the consequences of the road ahead. Adolescence is one of these rites of passage we traverse in life. This mother shows us the pitfalls for our preparation for young womanhood, marriage, parenthood, life, and so forth. Are you ready for this?

My historical Mother Wit is Fa Mulan. This ancient heroine was able to outwit a man's army for her entire twelve years of service and fulfill her family's obligation to their nation. She secretly challenged the status quo of her time and lived to return a hero. My personal Mother Wit came in my life as a part of my sisters' circle at a time of great personal turmoil, transitioning through divorce, my son's adolescence, and my remarriage. Alake was key to my soul searching, but she was only with me for that short cycle of my life. The way of her wisdom remains a part of me.

Lawyer Mother

Lawyer Mother is our advocate. She holds our confidences yet also holds us accountable. Her counsel is thoughtful, just, and wise. Her advice is meaningful. She builds us up when our confidence is shaken, giving straightforwardness in our confusion. She gives us sound judgment but is nonjudgmental. She is our light in the darkness. She is our quiet in the eye of the storm.

Teenage and young adult years are an intense period of decision making. Our parents and families have made choices for us in the past, but now we must sink or swim on our own. We need a counselor, whether we acknowledge it or not. There are man's laws to adhere to as well as the laws of nature and the universe. Morality, ethics, and integrity are the principles this mother seeks to help us live by. She is the manifestation of walking in righteousness. She is our supporter and guide to establish justice in our sphere of the world. She helps us stand up for ourselves against intimidation, oppression, and maltreatment.

My historical Lawyer Mother left the earth to enter the ancestral realm as I had just started writing this book. She advocated for us with her words—prose, stories, and poetry. She spoke for our hearts and minds. Maya Angelou is my Lawyer Mother. She is a truth teller. She is a voice. My girlfriend Nkechi Taifa is my personal Lawyer Mother. She's a friend and mother of my daughter's best friend. Our daughters raise us as we raise them. She happens to be a lawyer by profession, but she is my Lawyer Mother because of her advocacy for others.

Mentor Mother

> I stand where you think you want to be, but it is my shoulders that you need to stand on to look into a tomorrow I will never see.
>
> —Deborah L. Bernal M.D.

Mentor mother knows us better than we know ourselves. She tells us what we need to hear instead of what we want to hear. She supports us. She believes in us. She will rein us in when we are scattered and spread too thin. She gives us a gentle push to move us ahead. She will pull us up if we are stuck. She is our drill sergeant if necessary and our coach all the time. She is fair. She cheers us on.

We are facing the mountain our Mentor Mother has climbed, and she knows the terrain. She can help us avoid the pitfalls and suggest an easier route. She may need to toughen us up for the journey. She gives us the confidence to face the mountain fearlessly and to challenge our status quo. We can easily fall into bad habits that thwart our progress, but her guidance and confidence in us give us stability. She is a rock we can lean on to catch our breath up the steep terrain. We are on a mission, our life mission, fulfilling our divine purpose. Whether it is in our career or in our volunteer activities, this mother helps us to fulfill our destiny.

The Mentor Mother I resonate with from history is Madame Marie Curie. While I don't plan to get any Nobel Prize or be a research scientist, I am inspired by her shero's journey. She faced incredible odds and managed to obtain recognition as a scientist and a scholar far beyond the women of her time. She broke the glass ceiling with a quiet resolve and incredible determination. Hanna Sanders, M.D., is my personal shero. This Mentor Mother was my guide during a critical point in my medical career as I was choosing my specialty. Her example and advice helped to propel my professional career and volunteer service in our professional medical association. I feel so grateful to have this outstanding role model and mentor in my life.

Sexy Mama

Our Sexy Mama knows how to put an outfit together. She stays in shape for physical prowess as well as vanity. She looks good and feels good, and she is always prepared with a witty remark, a flirtatious tease, and gregarious laughter. She is a fun loving person and much fun to be around, but when we are young, she embarrasses us. We do not know quite how to handle her. We finally figure out she is too hot to be handled. She understands and knows how to use her feminine wiles. She lives life with passion and appreciation. There is a magic and a mystery. We grow to embrace her.

It is hard to identify with Sexy Mama until our full womanhood unfolds. She is our guide for romance. She is sexy, sensual, and erotic, and around her all of our senses are stimulated. The sounds, the sights, the smells, the tastes, and the pleasures of life are her fortress. She is the vessel of passion. She holds the emotions that inspire our dreams. She holds the creative spark of marriage, childbirth, and fertility. The energy of her life force is the spark of conception. This mother helps us to contact with our feminine energy. Unbridled, this force could have us drunk with pleasure. Our Sexy Mama shows us how to bring out, cultivate, and focus this energy so it does not consume us.

I have always felt the rhythm in my soul and have fancied myself a dancer. Therefore, it is no wonder my Sexy Mama figure is the incomparable Josephine Baker. Her life lessons range from the extremes of sensual and sexual energy, material wealth and poverty, and fame and abandonment. I was both lucky and unlucky to have my birth mother as my Sexy Mama. I adored her as a child, was embarrassed by her as a teenager, and admired her as an adult. I was blessed to be raised by this wonderful, sensual woman.

Warrior Mother

Warrior Mother offers the fierce protection of the lioness for her cubs. She is vigilant. She sleeps with one eye open and has eyes in the back of her head. Her instincts are sharp. Her sense of smell is keen. Her ears are perked. She can sense fear or danger. When we go out into the world away from her, she surrounds us with bubbles of light, love, and protection. She keeps our home a safe refuge. Her focus is protection. She lets us feel safe and secure because we are sure she has our back.

This assertive and, if need be, aggressive energy of motherhood is required for the protection and cultivation of the next generation. But there is a difference between mothering and smothering. Warrior Mother knows how to protect us and allow us to roam. This is the balancing act she deals with to empower the next generation. She knows we have to learn how to go out in the world and fend for ourselves. Overprotection weakens us, but this mother wants to make us strong. She wants us to be competent and confident. She wants to move our lineage forward. She understands Ashanti proverbs from Ghana: "The ruin of a nation begins in the homes of its people." That is not going to be her home. Her mothering is moving the nation and humanity forward.

From elementary school I was enthralled by the shero's journey of Joan of Arc. This young seventeen-year-old maiden moved her nation to restore its sovereignty. She's a powerful figure of faith, courage, and sacrifice. It is no wonder she is my historical Warrior Mother. On a personal note, my daughter guided me to my choice for the Warrior Mother in my private life. That person is her stepmother, whose trusted love and selfless protection might have saved my daughter's life.

Grandmother Mother

Our Grandmother Mother sees the little girl in us. She encourages our play and exploration. She brings us joy and happiness. The sweetness of her unconditional love is like our favorite dessert, but guiltless. We know that we are blessed; we know we are worthy by the look in her eyes. She will not let us get away with anything. She seems to know what is up before it even happens. As she keeps a loving eye on us, we feel the loads of appreciation. It is an ancestral love that goes beyond the generations. It lasts beyond time.

It takes the insight and experience of middle age to bring this grandmother into her fullness. She is slowing down into menopause and a positive change of life. She gracefully embraces this stage of life and uses it as a backdrop for planning, patience, and understanding limitation and heading into living an organized and structured life. If we let her guide us and we are willing to do the heavy lifting, together we can do great things. Often in youth we feel we know everything and our elders have nothing to share. We could learn so much from just observing our grandmothers "grandmothering" our children. We can learn how to fulfill our life's mission in a new way with the transition to this stage in life.

As I experience the gray hair and character-defining facial lines of this age, I've come to appreciate the life of my historical Grandmother Mother, Grandma Moses. When this elder could no longer, due to her physical limitations, express her artistic passion for needlepoint, she started a painting career at the age of seventy that spanned over three decades and gave her success beyond her wildest dreams. I chose my personal Grandmother Mother as a young wife and mother living far from my natal family. Mama Edna Derricks, an esteemed elder in my community, shared the warmth of home and family with my children and me and an entire community.

Queen Mother

Our Queen Mother is an inspiring and empowering role model. Her courage makes us fearless. Her leadership makes us strong. We watch her. We look up to her. We model her behavior. She can step out front to lead or lead by bringing up the rear. No matter where she is or what she is doing, she is regal. She cleans the toilet bowl with a crown. Yet she looks down on no one and holds compassion in her heart for all. She is up- to- date and modern but open to the wisdom of the ages. She is a constant force and unwavering. She is the matriarch of her family lineage. She guides the future leaders of her nation.

This mother is our fearless leader. She is guided by soul wisdom and knowing with an open heart. She is a spiritual messenger. There is a South African proverb, "The hand that rocks the cradle rules the nation and its destiny." This mother is first and foremost the ruler of herself. She knows who she is. She understands her destiny and embodies it. She has a spiritual message to bring to us to help us understand and embrace our destiny. She is willing to lead us, to assist us and set us on our way.

It is no wonder that I chose my namesake, the prophetess Deborah, as my Queen Mother. This ancient biblical figure is one of the few women prominent in the Old Testament. She was the fourth of the twelve Judges that ruled over the Hebrew people for many years of peace and wise stewardship. My personal Queen Mother is Madame Fatou Seck. Like Deborah, who gave counsel under the palm tree, people came far and wide to seek the guidance of this Queen Mother. I had the good fortune to receive her counsel during her trip from Senegal to the United States. Her advice changed my life forever.

Godmother Mother

The title of godmother is bestowed upon a trusted friend who will support her godchildren from their cradle to the grave. We look for a woman who is intuitive. She knows what to say and when to say it. She knows what to do and when to do it. She is in the world but not of it. Her realm is a higher plane of existence. She speaks with clarity. She speaks for the ears of those who are listening. She is comfortable with the mystery of life and flows within it as a blessed gift. Inside her there is a stillness, peace, and faith.

Our Godmother Mother gives us a shoulder to cry on. She stands by us in our grief. She is ever present in voiceless camaraderie. This comforts us when we are sad, carries us when we are weak, and holds us up when we are in despair. We cling to her when we are afraid, and she holds us in the safety of her bosom. She is a quiet, patient, ever-present guiding grace with a down pouring of hope. With this love, we are unbounded and feel all possibilities. With this love, we can accomplish anything.

If I could have chosen a godmother from all of the history, it would be Harriet Tubman. Her intention, thoughts, words, and deeds are the acts of a legendary figure. This Godmother Mother is an icon of the freedom we all should enjoy. I was fortunate in my college years to have been granted my best friend's mother, Connie Barber, as my Godmother Mother. Though she has made her final transition, her love remains in my heart forever, called to my memory with a comforting frequency.

These are the mothers in my Mothers' Council. I need them to further my spiritual growth. I need their loving counsel to guide me in aligning my intentions with my thoughts, attitudes, beliefs, behaviors, energy, efforts, emotions, speech, actions, lifestyle, and relationships to gain understanding and wisdom. I need them to assist me with the challenges I am facing in my daily life as well as the transitions of my lifecycles.

Chapter 2

EARTH MOTHER

IT BAFFLES ME AT TIMES when patients proclaim to me, "I do not have any stress." I am not sure which world they're living in, but it is not mine! There is a physical stress just to raise our body against gravity to get out of bed in the morning. There is the stress of hunger and thirst. We have the benefit in the Western world of going to the refrigerator and looking for something to eat that we purchased from the grocery store. Just think of generations ago when there was no grocery store and we had to plant and harvest our own food or hunt and kill it for ourselves. Today's struggle is what to choose to eat at the refrigerator or better yet down the grocery aisle. Will we give into our cravings and addictions or eat what is good for us? Will our food be fighting us back? Or can we not eat *that* food and avoid that pill altogether? Do we know we'll pay later in the waistline but still pack it away anyway? That is just food. We have not even talked about the stress of shelter, clothing, transportation, etc.

It is our struggles with earthly existence that motivate and awaken our spiritual power and creativity. We must learn how to function within natural law or pay the consequences. Physical resources we take for granted, such as the air in our atmosphere, the warmth of the sun, fertility of the land, and the moisture of the rain, are Mother Earth's gifts to us. Consistent adherence to natural law is essential for success. We require food, water, oxygen, sleep, and shelter. We have need of physical resources for this modern existence to progress our undertakings, including money, labor, capital, energy, family, and friends.

Humans have a long gestational and developmental period. We rely on our family members for our survival to adulthood. We are hardwired for reproduction and procreation through our hormonal system. These same hormones allow us to bond and nurture our offspring. What we want for our children is a fulfilled and gratified life experience. We want to thrive and not just survive. We want to empower them and for them to build upon how far we have been able to reach. This may require tough love at times and the ability for us to say no, let go, and let them fly versus hold them up or hold on to them. Our Earth Mother does not have that struggle. She allows surrender naturally, without attachment to the outcome. She knows all is well and in order.

Modern life provides a lot of options. We are being marketed to all the time. It is easy to get swept away with emotions that make us insecure. Earth Mother can help us when we want to avoid or deny unpleasant feelings and emotions. If we are unsure of ourselves in the spectacle of man's productions, we can seek quiet time to go into nature. Plant a garden in Mother Earth's rich, black, fertile soil to become grounded and rooted by the harmony and ecology of the life cycle of our plants. Anxious? Go to the mountaintop and breathe the clean, fresh air. Practice deep-breathing exercises, and feel the freedom of the expanse. Feeling defeated? Rise like the phoenix out of the ashes using the energy of a ritual fire to symbolically burn the regrets of the past to create the power for our present and all potential for our future. Feeling toxic? Go to the water for cleansing, healing, and rejuvenation.

Mother Earth

Mother Earth

Mother Earth was born 4.5 billion years ago. It took the majority of those billions of years for the earth to become inhabitable by humankind. Life began 3.8 billion years ago but humans only one hundred thousand years ago. Language was first recorded less than five thousand years ago. We are still truly Earth Mother's babies. She gives us food and shelter. She provides all the resources we need for a livelihood. She provides this stage for our fulfilling our destiny. What a great mom!

My goal is to live in harmony with Mother Nature's orderly, loving, universal intelligence. Life is movement. The one thing we can always count on is change. Matter and energy are always in a state of transformation. Humankind is evolving. Thought moves humanity forward. Progress is made on the leading edge of thought. Nature calls for us to adapt to change. Unsatisfied with our life? Change our thoughts, change our behavior. Mother Earth has confirmed this intuitive knowing through my observations.

To be in harmony with Mother Nature is to be in harmony with the cycles of life, life rhythms and vibrations, relationships, and life's contradictions.

Day-night cycles are important clues to living in balance. Until modern energy produced light, humanity got more sleep. We slept more in the winter and less during the summer months. Now our hormones are imbalanced from being off our day-to-day rhythm. Not to mention the sugar, carbs, caffeine, nicotine, medications, alcohol, and late-night entertainment keeping us up and leading to stress and disease. We are grown children and have choices to make. When it is dark, our Earth Mother wants us to go to sleep!

> To everything there is a season, and a time to every purpose under heaven.
>
> —Ecclesiastes 3:1MEV

We all have purpose. Mother Earth wants us to manifest our purpose for our lifetime. She wants us to be in tune with the flow of our life. Swimming upstream may be required at times to build strength and endurance while following our natural instincts. However, most of the time the appropriate rhythm is to go with the flow. There is a process for manifestation. The instant gratification that modernity provides relies on the benefits of others' manifestations that have come before us. It can hypnotize us, keeping us from our own creative work. Mother Earth is fertile and creative. We are her children and are meant to create.

Seasons are another important cycle. Just as with gardening, our thoughts and ideas are like bulbs planted in fall. During the deep, dark cold of winter, they are suspended in pure potentiality, silence, meditation, insightfulness, and contemplation for the blooming in spring. We are conceptualizing, we are planning, we are visualizing, and we are fueling these thoughts with our emotion. Spring is a time of activity, planting, and reproduction. Our thoughts and ideas springing forth out of the darkness and into the light are our blossoming, organizing, and incorporating all the elements our ideas need to move the process along. Summer is the time of high transformative energy. This is the time of hard work, consistency, and persistence-- unrelenting energy to stay the course and make it happen. Fall the time of harvest. We reap the reward of our efforts when we give thanks to our lessons as well as our victories. And the cycle continues.

And what of each person's life cycle? In each life there are many cycles, minutes, hours, days, weeks, months, years, and generations. We are growing from conception in our mother's womb through childhood and adolescence. We are being conditioned through language and education but hopefully also allowed to be perceptive thinkers, ready to manifest our dreams. In adolescence to young adulthood, we are mating, matriculating, and choosing our life's work. We are looking more forward than back. In our midlife, we are building homes and families, community and nations. We are advising the young and caring for the old. We are straddling. In our eldership, we are evaluating, analyzing, and synthesizing our life and our legacy. We are looking back more than forward. We have so much to share, so little time. But it is time to be at peace for our final transition, to watch over our loved ones we leave behind. And the cycle continues.

> Nothing in life has any meaning except for the meaning that you give it.
>
> —Anthony Robbins

We use the principles of physics and the law of relativity every day on our global positioning system (GPS) to find out where we are. Our physical reality on Mother Earth allows us to compare and contrast our material universe. Nothing can be bad or good, big or small unless we compare it to something else. We can think about how things can be separated or divided and compartmentalized, or we can think about how things can be grouped, unified, and integrated. Morally we can fear, hate, divide, and conquer, or we can love, appreciate, unite, and celebrate. There is an old African proverb, "If you do not know where you were going, any road will take you there." We choose.

The law of vibration I learned in physics was different from the law of vibration I learned on the street. On the street I heard, "She has a good vibe!" In physics class I learned about movement and energy. Everything vibrates; nothing rests. There are various vibrational levels or frequencies. With matter, the lower the density, the higher the speed of vibration, and the higher the density, the lower the speed of vibration. Thoughts are vibrations. Our minds are both receivers and transmitters of vibrations. We must take time to evaluate our thoughts. Our hearts, our guts, and our nervous system are receivers. How do our thoughts, situations and circumstances, relationships, and decisions make us feel? What is our gut reaction? Does the thought of it make me have goose bumps? I am often asked my medical opinion as to whether I think that person should have a particular procedure or intervention. My advice is always the same: get as much information as you can for your head, but make your decision by running it through your heart. The wisdom of our body can give us much inner sight.

> Everything flows, out and in; everything has its tides; all things rise and fall; the pendulum-swing manifests in everything; the measure of the swing to the right is the measure of the swing to the left; rhythm compensates.
>
> —The Kybalion

Everything operates by rhythm—our heartbeat, our breath, our brain waves. The tide comes in and goes out, day follows night, the moon waxes and wanes, and life has its peaks and valleys. The waves of the ocean can be a calming hush, a roaring gale, or a devastating tsunami all part of the rhythm of life. We must deal with Mother Earth's natural forces and the forces we create with our thoughts, attitudes, beliefs, and behaviors. We can choose our intentions, words, and actions. We can create the rituals that provide the rhythm of our life, which ground us and hold us in good standing—bodily rituals like hygiene, physical rituals like exercise, and spiritual rituals like using nature as a guide, finding beauty, gratitude, and joyfulness in our everyday, ordinary existence. We create the rhythms of our life.

The law of cause and effect purports that this is an orderly universe. Things happen for a reason. Every cause has an effect, and every effect has its cause. In terms of physics, each action has an equal and opposite reaction. I learned it as, "What goes around, comes around" on the street and in church as a Golden Rule. "Do unto others as you would have them do unto you." (Luke 6:31 MEV). Intentions, thoughts, words, beliefs, actions, relationships, and lifestyle choices have consequences. It is our choice. If we do not like what we are getting (effect), we can change what we are giving (cause). Again, we have choice if we choose to exercise it.

Ecology is the maintenance of balance and harmony of all life on Mother Earth. It is an appreciation for the abundance and diversity of life and maintaining its integrity. It is an understanding that my body temple is a gift to be held holy, cared for, and valued. We understand that Mother Earth is a gift to all of us, to be held sacred, shared, cared for, and cherished. We keep our mind, body, and spirit clean and pure. We keep Mother Earth clean, the air, the water, and the environment. We maintain an environmental equilibrium to avoid waste, use what is needed, and replenish as we can. This endeavor cannot occur in isolation. We are all interdependent. We are all multifaceted, multidimensional, and intergenerational. We must all do our part on every level, personal, societal, governmental, political, and international. Together, we do make a difference.

I would love to advocate to the Supreme Court on behalf of Mother Earth. If a corporation can be declared a person, why can't she? I want to advocate for the ecology of our planet. It is a lesson she has tried to teach us that as a race we have not yet learned.

Allow health. Allow wealth. See money as energy. I've heard money referred to as "dirty" money, as if great wealth contains an inherent evil. But money is a tool for good or evil. We choose. Giving and receiving are the same energy, just the opposite poles of a cycle. Generosity is inherent to the resources Mother Earth shares with us, but it must be recycled and replenished, like the medicine wheel of the Native American tradition of the sacred cycle of life.

Sabrina Johnson

SABRINA JOHNSON

"The same thing makes you laugh, makes you cry" (southern proverb).

EARTH MOTHER SABRINA JOHNSON IS a Natural Woman, and with her I learn to be an Earth Mother—naturally. A simple administrative error prevented a young man from being caught behind enemy lines and returning to the United States in a body bag, as did his unit during the Korean War. This young man was spared and become Sabrina's father.

Sabrina reluctantly led the May Day Ceremony as a kindergartener as drum major. Initially, stage fright captured her, but she worked through it with much rehearsal and finally accepted her role with enthusiasm. She credits supportive feedback from home and extended family, church, school, and the community helping her. The "village experience" cultivating her sense of self-confidence.

Seeds Planted Early

Sabrina was searching for an answer to racism from a very young age. She noticed differences in behavior, how people are treated, financial resources, and perceptions with respect to black people and white people. Whether from teachers or classmates, school was a significant setting for observing and experiencing the hardship of racism. Then, in her early adolescence, a life-changing event occurred. The father of a classmate/friend was lynched very close to Sabrina's home in their small hometown of Aiken, South Carolina. He was a skilled, hardworking, responsible, extraordinarily handsome black man/husband/father of four children—the last one having been born just a couple of weeks before his murder. There were no charges filed and no thorough investigation. A rumor circulated about him and a white woman who worked at a store near the wooded area where his body was found. Sabrina was extremely disturbed that none of the black leadership in the town, including preachers, school officials, leaders of community organizations, and even her parents, seemed to do anything about it. There were no protests. People still went to work. Everything seemed to stay in order as usual. She was angry, disappointed, and confused.

She was perplexed and needed to make sense of that killing and all the multitude of racist experiences she had as a child and those she read about. The mistreatment continued despite her excelling academically and in moral character. She and her classmates were constantly bumping into racial barriers. Interestingly, this also enhanced her love of science because there was a purity in science. Sabrina realized that things make sense by understanding how things work. Her love of science and its application continued and she eventually became a chemical engineer.

A Search for Meaning

After a minor car accident in her early twenties, Sabrina followed the voice within and took time out to go to the mountains and reflect on why the incident occurred. She was not at fault in the accident. She spent the weekend reading, journaling, dreaming, deeply thinking, and feeling downloads of insights. A theme of transformation emerged and set forth four priorities as her guideposts she has followed in life: health, nutrition, and fitness; connection to history and culture; understanding racism; and spirituality with exploration through indigenous perspectives.

Health, Nutrition, and Fitness

> Balance is my thing!
>
> Her nutrition comes from a plant-based dietary lifestyle, mostly raw, consuming foods as close to their natural state as possible to remain healthy and fit. Her fitness activities include Kemetic and other styles of yoga, African dance, step aerobics, aquatics, kickboxing, and strength training. She honors the natural medicine of movement as well as stillness—all with the connection to earth energy. She epitomizes balance. She resonates with the yin yang symbol. I selected to draw her picture in toe stand as it reflects the true nature of her character.
>
> —Sabrina Johnson

She recently took her goddaughter Afryea to a Zumba class with a high-energy, hard-core belly dancer turned Zumba teacher. While Afryea at twenty-one panted and struggled to keep up and had to take breaks, she noticed that her godmother did not take breaks and was a top performer in the class. Afryea was astonished that at the end of class that her godmother was not even winded. Blessed with having no adverse health conditions or need for medications, Sabrina's vitality is visible. She glows radiating health. She has read a lot of books and attended health retreats and lectures, but her true guidance comes from tuning into her inner voice. She finds this superior to conventional medicine.

> Water. Sabrina loves the water.

Sabrina expresses unending gratitude for her mother's gift of extending ballet and swim lessons to Sabrina. The fluid movements learned in ballet enhanced her experience in the water. As a child, you couldn't drag Sabrina out of the ocean or pool. Her lifelong love affair with the water now includes recent certifications in aqua spin, as a lifeguard, and in SCUBA diving. Sabrina goes to the water for restoration, rejuvenation, and inspiration.

The ocean provides a whole different perspective, with different natural laws governing life on land and in the water. The buoyancy of water in opposition to the forces of gravity is a metaphor for staying afloat and being lifted up when being oppressed. She marvels at the Grand Canyon and notes, "Water did that!" Water is the universal solvent—a metaphor for the capacity to incorporate a wide spectrum of interests and abilities and manifest them as needed in different situations. Water is the original birthplace of life and is essential for life on our earth. At birth we emerge from our gestation from the water in the womb.

Tranquility and power also characterize the energy associated with another very important influence in Sabrina's life. She was at a Kemetic Yoga/raw food retreat on the beach in Jamaica. She saw a striking woman in the distance with a tremendous presence that, in addition to being visually evident, could be felt. Sabrina met her and visited her wellness spa, Jackie's on the Reef, a healing resort on the ocean in Negril, Jamaica. It mesmerized her right away with the beauty and positive vibrations. This magical place is now a refuge for her, and her relationship with Jackie Lewis came at the time of her search for a Spiritual Mother. A key part of her wellness is taking the time to fellowship, relax, renew, and rejuvenate herself cradled in the healing cultivated in Jackie's oasis of nature. To her it is like returning to the womb. Immersion in nature and nurturing feeling cosmically attuned are the gifts at this incredible corner of paradise. Freshly grown garden vegetables and fruits, sunshine, serenity, extraordinary spa treatments, breathtaking sunsets, star gazing, and great snorkeling compels her to return again and again.

Mother Earth

Sabrina loves Mother Earth, nature, and science and has been using her reasoning skills to answer questions, compel analysis, and problem solve to care for Mother Earth. As a chemical engineer she left private industry to be on the leading edge of environmental progress. Her policy analysis and regulatory work at the EPA is fulfilling. Keenly aware of the interdependence of all life, she embodies a holistic lifestyle, caring for herself, humankind, and the planet. She finds comfort and healing in indigenous ties to nature through native healing practices, such as the sweat lodge and spiritual spirit-filled African dance and drumming. Beauty and order of nature is balanced through harmony in relationships with ourselves, others, and the planet.

Culture and History

In fifth grade learning about Egypt and Egyptians, she intuitively knew that these were black people. In seventh grade she read a book about the pyramids and wrote her first term paper about their power. She knew one day she would go there and she participated in a study tour of Egypt led by Tony Browder. She has embarked on a journey of self-directed study to learn about African history and culture since she was not taught about it in school. Self-love and self-esteem are lost on generations because of this lack of knowledge. Sabrina helped to fill this gap by teaching African history and values at a Saturday school for at-risk girls that she and friends pioneered. She continues to study and share, traveling nationally and internationally. There is a benefit in Sankofa—going back to fetch the lessons of our collective past that can be applied to benefit our global future. She has found that the "new age" is just a step back to living old-school style.

Understanding Racism

> If you understand a thing, you know how to relate to it.
>
> —Dr. Frances Cress Welsing

When she read the book *The Isis Papers* and heard Dr. Frances Cress Welsing speak, she knew she had found her Melanin-Minded Mother. The clarity of Dr. Welsing's *Cress Theory of Color Confrontation and Racism (White Supremacy)* made a linkage with Sabrina's explorations of that quintessential question, "Why?" concerning racism. She could now make sense of "inexplicable" behaviors. The clarity and logic impressed her. Sabrina always had questions, and Dr. Welsing had answers. Always teacher and student, they also became like mother and daughter. Sabrina traveled with Dr. Welsing. Sabrina also hosted gatherings with Dr. Welsing regularly. She was never star struck by her brilliance but was keenly aware of the amazing person she was. Dr. Welsing's life unfolded to enable her to figure out the underlying motivations that fuel the system of white supremacy. The most important was her encountering Mr. Neely Fuller Jr. Together, Dr. Welsing and Mr. Fuller gave the world the *keys to the colors.*

A devoted student of the Cress Welsing Institute for over twenty-five years Sabrina is now a leading voice in protecting and preserving Dr. Welsing's legacy. She was blessed to be at her bedside in Dr. Welsing's final hours with an immense sense of gratitude for having her in her life. Sabrina finds comfort in the completeness of their relationship. Nothing left unsaid. Sabrina received a blueprint, map, and compass for navigating the voyage to justice for peace on the planet. Dr. Welsing's harvest included the security that her legacy will continue through her student. Sabrina feels empowered to amplify Dr. Welsing's body of work and finish the task at hand.

Spirituality

Healing Her Mother-Daughter Relationship

Sabrina's mother exemplifies devotion to parenting and integrity. Her mother's guidance, vision, character, and fiercely protective posture were a blessing in shaping her development. A big-time daddy's girl, Sabrina embraces the tremendous imprint her mother put on her. At times, though, her mother was smothering. Her mother's fears were in conflict with Sabrina's fearless sense of adventure. Numerous incidents occurred over the years and escalated to a crossroads in their relationship. As an adult, she decided to confront her mother to resolve the issues that had arisen between them over the years—or at least air her grievances in a very deliberate way. This was an extremely difficult decision. Her mother could be quite stubborn and argumentative. Sabrina had played out many scenarios in her head about the upcoming confrontation. Sabrina laid out the problems. She expected resistance, denial, and arguments but was stunned and speechless by her mother's simple apology. It was not at all anticipated, and it even took Sabrina a while to process it.

Sabrina's approach to confronting her mother was grounded in the understanding that her mother's intentions were unquestionably in the best interest of Sabrina's development. Perhaps that context of appreciation motivated the spirit of apology and reconciliation. Sabrina emerged aware of her own enormous nurturing capacity. Able to forgive and appreciate her mother, Sabrina experienced a transformative insight. The why became more important than how her mother related to her! Years later there was a role reversal. Due to illness, Sabrina functioned in the role of mother in caring for her mother. They experienced high-drama in which Sabrina had to take actions that her mother heavily resented at the time. However, the highest good did prevail, and understanding, forgiveness, and appreciation surfaced once again this time flowing in the other direction.

Extending the Healing: Mother-Son Relationship

Sabrina used her nurturing capacity and her forgiveness experience to help heal my son Hasani's and my relationship. He was twenty-five years old at the time, and we had been estranged since his rambunctious, rebellious teenage years, largely in reaction to my divorce from his father. She was the peacemaker of our issues arising from my parenting in his childhood. She acts as a mediator for the court system and broadened her skills to mediate domestic disputes of the heart. She had us answer a series of questions to unearth our feelings, thoughts, actions, and reactions around the issues of our past. She allowed us to come together openly to bear witness to each other's journey and both empathize with the other. She worked us through a healing process that allowed us to bring closure to wounds we had left open for years. We both apologized, and we both forgave ourselves and were forgiven by each other. We now have a strong adult child and parent relationship that we have both grown up to embrace.

Reconnecting Kindred Spirits

While Sabrina has had no biological children, she has generations of stepchildren and grandchildren, godchildren, little sisters, and big sister friends like myself that she mothers. Sabrina was under my care as a patient and happened to be at another appointment in the office building just before my daughter Afryea's first birthday ritual blessing. Spirit brought Sabrina at the right place at the right time, and although she was not on the guest list, she was able to stay when I asked. Afryea arrived in the arms of her godmother, but she made her way walking across the room to grab Sabrina's leg and indicated that she wanted to get picked up by her. Babies are attuned to spirit. Observe them carefully. Watch where they lead. Afryea stayed with Sabrina throughout the entire event and didn't want to have anything to do with anyone else—including myself and her father. It was apparent to everyone that a divine connection was renewed. They have been deeply connected since. At Afryea's request at eight years old, we filled out the paperwork for Sabrina to officially be documented as her godmother. Sabrina's motherly nurturing and support have continued with Afryea's older brother, Hasani as well.

> With an *open* mind your *heart* will open. Once the Path is revealed the way forward becomes clear and all you will need will be fulfilled.
>
> —Sabrina Johnson

As Dr. Welsing was approaching her acute medical condition, Sabrina knew nothing of it consciously but spiritual praise songs were priming her for the journey ahead. Before even knowing of Dr. Welsing's impending death, she had made acupuncture and massage appointments that she needed to get her through all the activities surrounding her transition rites, rituals, death, and memorials. She knows where to go to get the assistance she needs to confront life challenges. She has access to the healer/warriors she needs to transcend any obstacles.

I admire this prosperity consciousness in my Earth Mother. When I was physically, morally, and financially bankrupt from the changes in the healthcare industry strangling the healing work of my solo medical practice, she bankrolled me to keep me afloat as I made various transitions. She waited patiently as I was able to reorganize and pay her back. I am forever grateful for the confidence and patience she showed. Money issues between friends have been known to destroy friendships. She showed me kindness, trust, and abundance. She is a role model of philanthropy. I try now to pay that forward.

Enjoy an Integrated Wholeness

Sabrina quite separate from my endeavor writing this book developed her own ancestral council to engage for situations she encounters in all aspects of her life. She does not get caught up in the person or the personalities. After all, we are all human. She keeps focused on her mission, doesn't take things personally, and makes this ancestral connection active to carry out the unfinished business the ancestors left for us to push forward. She is truly my Earth Mother who is busy self-mothering and animating her own personal motto: "Adding fulfillment to the lives I touch."

Sabrina shows us how living naturally gives us security within ourselves and also makes us sure about our lives. Living a holistic life includes developing a livelihood to sustain our existence but also nourishing and supporting our soul. This Earth Mother shows us how to conduct our lives in a particular manner leading to a positive and satisfying existence for us and our community. We can enjoy our lives and make life choices that sustain good relationships with positive energy. She shows us how to enthusiastically explore our interest, increasing our vitality, keeping us active and our life meaningful with contributions to the general welfare and well-being of society. What a wonderful woman to have in my life.

Chapter 3

Doctor Mom

Doctor Mom knows first and foremost she is responsible for her own healing. She can only do her healing work from a position of her own healing power—self-healing. She has a personal relationship with healing. Through this she has made the way to heal others.

Healing is an endless process that we open ourselves up to experience. She is aware of and not afraid of the fact that suffering may be the catalyst leading to healing. Often illnesses of the body are the impetus for a soul overhaul. However, most of us don't want to do the work and don't want to wait for the results. We want a force outside of ourselves to fix us, and we want it to have happened yesterday. The real work requires transforming suffering into spiritual transformation.

Doctor Mom is helping us identify our true nature as opposed to conforming, controlling, and assimilating. Breath is essential to life, yet we quickly learn to go against nature. We are taught the stomach in and chest out to breathe. Look at how a baby breathes. They have natural instincts that will allow deep diaphragmatic abdominal breathing. We need to relearn how to breathe. This helps give us stability and clarity. Her healing involves restoring our sanity and mental clarity. She does so gently. We must face our own healing from a position of our own power. Only then are we positioned to help others.

The Healing Attunement

How do we become attuned to the healing energy? With kindness and caring; with compassion and love for self and others; by taking responsibility for the nature and quality of our social interactions; and by seeing all people for their godliness. We assume all people are children of God, and this is central to the core of our healing philosophy. This allows a guidance that is divinely inspired. It allows the healer to be available to all possibilities. This provides the direction for right choices relative to our needs and the correct methods relative to our deeds.

> If you are not a part of the solution you are part of the problem.
>
> —Eldridge Cleaver

Just like the roads need to be quiet in the middle of the night to do road repair, our homes and lifestyles must be tranquil to promote our healing. This mother provides that protection and that sacred healing space for us to lay our burdens down and strip ourselves naked, able to bear our souls in a truly unjudged confession.

Mother Teresa

Mother Teresa

> Blessed are the peacemakers, for they shall be called the sons of God.
>
> —Matthew 5:9 MEV

Agnes Gonxha Bojaxhiu was eight years old when her father was killed and left her family financially devastated. He had been a self-made successful businessman who was caught between the feud of warring religious and political factions in Albania. He took no sides but helped all those in need. His philosophy: Where revenge, I bring forgiveness. Her mother was now a single mother of three, with Agnes being the youngest. She sold textiles and handmade embroidery to make money. Daily prayers together and yearly pilgrimages solidified her family and their values. She knew love because it began in her home.

> This I command you: that you love one another.
>
> —John 15:17 MEV

At twelve years old, she felt a call to become a nun. She helped her mother organize church events, walked with her mother to hand out food and supplies to the poor, and sang in the choir. Over the next five years, she contemplated and researched and eventually determined she wanted to do mission work in India. She left home at eighteen years old and never returned or saw her family members again. Had she returned, she would have never been allowed to leave. She began her training in Ireland in the Loreto order of nuns. She completed her first vows two years later while working in India. She was stuck teaching within the convent walls until age twenty-five. With special permission to teach out of the convent, she completed her final vows two years later and became Mother Teresa. Within a very short time, she became the principal of another convent school and was for nine years again restricted to live within the convent walls.

> We know that all things work together for good to those who love God, to those who are called according to His purpose.
>
> —Romans 8:28 MEV

September 10, 1946, is celebrated annually as an inspiration day when Mother Teresa received what she described as "a call within a call." She was told to leave the convent and help the poor by living among them. She petitioned for two years before she was allowed to follow her call to give hope to those who have lost it and to see the face of the Lord in all who suffer.

> "Have deep compassion for the people. People are suffering much, very, very much; mentally, physically, in every possible way, and so I think we are there to bring that hope, that love, that kindness … A carrier of God's love, the love of an infinite thirsty God."[1]
>
> —Mother Teresa

> Therefore my heart is glad, and my glory rejoices; my flesh also will rest in security.
>
> —Psalm 16:9 MEV

With the true love of God, Mother Teresa was confident in her security to travel among the people she wished to serve. Dressed in

[1] The writing of Mother Teresa of Calcutta © by the Mother Teresa Center, exclusive licensee throughout the world of the Missionaries of Charity for the works of Mother Teresa. Used with permission.

white cotton saris lined with three blue stripes along its edge, white for purity and blue for the Virgin Mary, she left the convent. She first spent several weeks in a medical mission to learn some basic medical knowledge. At thirty-eight years old, in December of 1948, all alone she ventured out into the slums of Calcutta.

> The Lord bless you and keep you; the Lord make His face to shine upon you, and be gracious unto you; the Lord lift His countenance upon you, and give you peace.
>
> —Numbers 6:24–26 MEV

She gained the confidence of the children with her smile. Her smile radiated the peace and love in her heart. Mother Teresa's inroads into the community started by her teaching small children on the street, using a stick to draw in the dirt. She began visiting children's families and offering medical information. People began to hear of her work and gave her donations. She did what she could and was contented to know that whatever she was able to do was meaningful. Even small things can make a big impact in a person's life.

> My soul waits in silence on God alone; from Him comes my salvation.
>
> —Psalm 62:1 MEV

Her first helper arrived in 1949, and soon after ten other former students came to serve with her. By the end of her provisional period, she petitioned to form a new order of nuns, the Missionaries of Charity. Her request was granted by Pope Pius XII on October 7, 1950. Their mission is to give wholehearted free service to the poorest of the poor. This order of nuns spends time in silent contemplation on the sacred heart of Jesus Christ.

> Love suffers long and is kind; love envies not; love flaunts not itself and is not puffed up.
>
> —1 Corinthians 13:4 MEV

In her confessions and writings, she repeatedly asked for prayers for the torments during her "dark night of the soul" that lasted for almost her entire fifty-year ministry in the gutters of India. She complained of deep down emptiness and darkness, wondering where her faith was. It was in the same spirit of Christ Jesus asking from the cross, "My God, My God, why have You forsaken Me?" (Mark 15:34 MEV). This is considered a passive purification. This doubt never stopped her determination. Was it merely empathy from working with those who had no hope? Did those lost, forgotten, and abandoned souls touch the feeling of emptiness in her own soul? Was it a passive purification of her soul? She stated on the subject of suffering, "When you go to the poor and see them suffering and come back home you feel you need the penance to share the suffering of Christ. Let us pray for all the grace we need to unite our sufferings to His, that many souls, who live in darkness and misery, may know His love and life."[2] And so she did help others as she suffered. She, and all the nuns of the Missionaries of Charity, spent many hours devoted to prayer.

Mother Teresa believed that little things went a long way. She saw people in such a terrible rush in modern life to get ahead financially, but they had little time for each other. This disruption in the relationships at home begins that disruption of peace between the people in the world. The elders and infirmed were abandoned and neglected. She opened the Place of the Immaculate Heart, a home for the dying where terminally ill would be fed and bathed and given the opportunity to die with dignity and the rituals of their faith.

---

[2] ibid

> But Jesus called them to Him and said, "Permit the little children to come to Me, and do not hinder them. For to such belongs the kingdom of God"
>
> —Luke 18:16 MEV

A children's home provided medical care and housed, educated, and fed orphans. If not adopted, the children there learned a skilled trade and found marriage partners. God did provide for these services through donations that often occurred on a daily basis to fulfill the needs of the day. She did not turn children away and was often criticized for the conditions at the homes she established. But she put forth the effort, and God found a way to make it work for the good of all. Every small gift was appreciated and used. Together every small gift was able to do great things for the community. Children show the beauty of God's love.

> "The moment I pick up a person who is hungry, give him a plate of rice, I've removed the hunger. But the person who is hurt, who is lonely, who feels rejected, unwanted, unloved—I think that's the much greater poverty, much greater disease."[3]
>
> —Mother Teresa

The leprosy crisis was hampered by widespread fear of lepers. She eventually created a Leprosy Fund and a Leprosy Day to educate the public and established mobile clinics. After a trip to the holy land in the mid-1960s, she was able to establish a leper colony called the Place of Peace where the lepers could live and work. Before the tenth anniversary of the Missionaries of Charity, they were given permission to establish other houses in India.

---

[3] ibid

> Give, and it will be given to you: Good measure, pressed down, shaken together, and running over will men give unto you. For with the measure you use, it will be measured unto you.
>
> —Luke 6:38 MEV

By the fifteenth anniversary, they were able to establish houses outside India and soon became worldwide. International recognition for her work followed with numerous honors, including the Nobel Peace Prize in 1979. Humble, she never took personal credit, saying, "I am nothing but a little pencil in the hand of God. It is He who writes, it is He who thinks, it is He who decides."[4] She never measured her giving. It was through intense love that she was able to continue to give.

> Meekness, and self-control; against such there is no law.
>
> —Galatians 5:23 MEV

With recognition also comes controversy. She had been criticized for having substandard conditions in her houses for the ill and dying, no proper medical training, and trying to convert these vulnerable people to Christianity. She was admonished as she openly spoke out against abortion and birth control as tenants of her Catholic faith. Her critics, trying to use these means to stop overpopulation and the growth of poverty, wanted her support.

> But the fruit of the Spirit is love, joy, peace, patience, gentleness, goodness, faith.
>
> —Galatians 5:22 MEV

In the 1980s she opened Gift of Love Homes for AIDS sufferers.

---

4 ibid

Despite her increasing age and declining health, she continued to travel the world sharing her message of love, peace, and hope. Prior to her death, she was finally relieved of the long darkness and suffering. Mother Teresa was known to have spent long hours in mental prayer and through special readings to cultivate the gift of prayers that finally elevated her wounded spirit. This time, devoted to God in prayer, was her inexhaustible source of effective and loving service.

> "He says at the hour of death, you and I are going to be judged—not from what big things we have done, but what we have been to the poor: that hungry man, that man that came to our gate, that lonely person, that blind person passing through the street, that person so lonely, so unwanted, so unloved in my family right here … That is why whatever you do for each other in your family, Jesus takes it as done to him. And when we die and go home to God again, our Lord will judge us on this love."[5]
>
> —Mother Teresa

She died in 1997 of heart failure, leaving over four thousand Missionaries of Charity Sisters, in 610 centers, in 123 countries globally. Her ministry has continued to grow. Since Mother Teresa's death, the Vatican began the process to canonize her as a saint. Mother Teresa's Sainthood, September 4, 2016, was not without controversy. She was criticized in her lifetime as well as during her canonization process. However, most believe that all she did was motivated by love. While I do not believe in all she believed, I admire her conviction and commitment to those beliefs. I seek to emulate her compassion, faith, and hope despite the odds she faced. My father, a Jehovah's Witness, bled to death a week after open-heart surgery, refusing blood transfusion. I did not believe as he believed, but I admired his

[5] ibid

conviction. When he had the choice to live or die, he chose to die according to the beliefs he lived by.

> If I speak with the tongues of men and of angels, and have not love, I have become as sounding brass or a clanging cymbal. If I have the gift of prophecy, and understand all mysteries and all knowledge, and if I have all faith, so that I could remove mountains, and have not love, I am nothing. If I give all my goods to feed the poor, and if I give my body to be burned, and have not love, it profits me nothing.
>
> —1 Corinthians 13:1–3 MEV

Mother Teresa's mission to help the poorest of the poor was a calling to live her destiny, her life's work. I believe she was following her heart in what she did and how she did it. My mission does not take me to far-off places, or working with lives in desperation. My mission meets us in our routine existence in our own homes. My mission is to awaken the unconscious average person living in the Western modernity—me! To reconnect us to what we have disconnected from in modern life—nature and natural law, our own body, and becoming body aware, the junk food that is turning us into junk, the modern pleasures that distract us from ourselves and each other and prevent healthy relationships. We are living in the past or the future with no attention/connection to the present. We are unconscious of the choices we are making and what other choices are available to us for our healing, doing what is expected of us from others or just what we have been programed to do habitually and continue to do over and over again. It is a poverty of consciousness.

Pearl Taylor

Pearl Taylor

She is ninety-six years young, a bubble of love, joy, and enthusiasm, and her heart is as big as her smile. Her message has always been positive and powerful. She is my aunt Pearlie, my Doctor Mom. She got that title in my life because she taught me from a young age the key to healing: positivity. I learned to give hope to my patients from her example of love. She was new age in the 1960s before I knew what new age was. She taught me the value of a smile, a hug, and a laugh. She was a role model of a healing attitude, giving me her affirmations in words of wisdom before I knew what an affirmation was or had heard about the power of positive thinking. She was a living example of that for me. My mission to "heal and be healed" starts with my own self-healing. I lead by example, and she was a positive role model for me in that. I can only heal others by being an example of self-healing, and this book is one strategy I use to heal myself.

Pearl is a fitting name for this rare gem of a mother. Aunt Pearlie's journey started in Cuba in 1921. The middle daughter of five girls born to education-minded parents, they had an additional family home in Jamaica to facilitate the education of their girls. Her father continued to work in Cuba until 1963, visiting family on weekends and holidays.

From childhood she could sense the importance of her environment. She loved her home and family but enjoyed spending time with others. She visited friends' homes that had a fun and pleasant atmosphere. She enjoyed spending her holidays with other families looking for experiences that would provide diverse feelings for her to enjoy.

After high school she married my uncle Karl. He had immigrated to

Painesville, Ohio, after the war and was living in a rooming house and working in a factory. She left Jamaica at twenty-four with my infant cousin, Michael, to join her husband. The next day while her husband was at work, she and her son were evicted from the property. She went door to door in the black neighborhood of Painesville asking for a room to rent. She and her son were finally taken in by the only black doctor in town, Dr. Rucker. They stayed in a curtained-off hallway for a month until one of the apartments in the doctor's apartment building became available. The apartment had no heat. She wanted a home for her and her family. In Jamaica they were accustomed to owning their own homes and not renting.

She found a home for sale on Jefferson Street. It was three bedrooms, with a full basement, dining room, and formal living room. They wanted $4,500. Without credit or down payment they went to the bank. Unable to get a loan, my aunt Pearlie asked the lone officer if there was somebody rich who could help them. They asked Dr. Carmody for help. It still required a $200 bank loan for a deposit, but the doctor agreed to purchase the home in his name, allowing them to rent to own the home. They had another son and over the years brought fourteen families of friends and relatives over from Jamaica to Painesville. With the equity in their home, they were able to buy a larger home. Their family had been the foundation of a growing community. However, her world was rocked by their divorce. She was shocked and blamed herself. But looking back, it was a blessing in disguise. It opened her mind to new ways thinking.

Her struggles with her divorce led her to classes given by a local medical doctor and health food store owner. She changed her mind, and she awakened to her higher self. It gave her freedom. She remarried, and they attended classes together. She raised her children Catholic but left the Catholic Church, searching many denominations for a religious home, and was disillusioned by most. The spiritual discontent propelled their spiritual quest. They attended course work and sessions all over the country. She enjoyed being in stimulating environments with others seekers. Aunt Pearlie and her husband ended up in California with the Unity Church. Her husband got a job at UCLA. She volunteered for a publishing company. When she volunteered at a school library, they ended up offering her a job. They enjoyed themselves, and she felt like they were on a constant vacation. They stayed five years, and it was there they were introduced to *A Course in Miracles.*

Expand My Mind

The course has been a forty-year journey that she still continues today. They kept hearing about it and did get involved in it and began facilitating it once a week in their home with students. They would take seminars at colleges and a stay a week at a time. They did seminars for years all over the place. She remembers being shocked in Chicago when the course was being espoused by a Catholic priest. They became teachers of the course and in 1978 moved to Dayton, Ohio, to help her son and daughter-in-law with her two- and four-year-old granddaughters. She has had wonderful teachers over the years. She has been in groups to take the course to the prisons. She is doing the course by herself now and observing how the truth is evolving. She has made a commitment to heal the world.

> My mission is to help heal the world.
>
> —Pearl Taylor

When I asked my aunt Pearlie to share her wisdom, this is what she shared: "Love yourself. Happiness is about self-worth. Be good to yourself! It is important to know your higher self. The higher self gives us so much freedom. It gives the awareness of who I am. It gives the awareness of who others are. Be thoughtful of others. We are all so connected. How we think of others is how we think of ourselves. We each have the Christ within. Do not hold grudges! Bless others and hold them in the Christ consciousness, and ask that it come forth in them. Keep seeing the Christ in people and situations because it changes things and people."

Mental Discipline

She has learned that a life spent learning is a life well spent. She continues to spend many hours in journaling, quiet contemplation, and deep thought. She writes prayers for a divine mind. One of the most important lessons she has learned is positivity!

> Negativity holds things back despite strength and intelligence. People cannot find themselves. We have to learn how to change our thoughts forms. We are born into the thoughts forms around us. Do not deal with small talk! We can accept those thoughts forms, or we can seek new ways of thinking. By changing our mind we can discover ourselves. If we don't get bogged down in anything, we can find the reality is inside of us. We must look at life as possibilities. It helps!
>
> —Pearl Taylor

> Family is a gift. Couples have to grow together to get to God for a successful marriage and life. Give and you shall receive. It is all about giving. It is not all about money; it is the energy of giving service. Give in selfless service and you will never be broke.
>
> —Pearl Taylor

Spirit Is Ever Present

She enjoys family, friends, and travel. When she feels bad, she writes. When tragedy occurs, she has to send positive thoughts. She gets up and writes. She asks for divine order and harmony. She can make shifts right away. She doesn't let the mind control her. She does the work to shift her thinking. Her health regimen is one half lemon in a glass of water first thing in the morning, yoga, and walking.

> I can have a party by myself! I do, a lot.
>
> —Pearl Taylor

Aunt Pearlie is a thinker. She understands that all thought is a prayer offering, and she taught me the value of positive thought as positive prayer. She is compassionate and gives us hope for living a long and happy life, free from regret and despair. From her I've learned the importance of forgiving and letting go of negativity. The most important person for us to forgive is ourselves. If we are holding out forgiveness for ourselves, we will not have the compassion to truly forgive others.

Forgiveness is not an event; it is a process. I see four stages of forgiveness. There are four tenets to forgiving: give attention; give thanks; give love; and give back. When you do not feel good physically or emotionally, it is a wakeup call to give attention to what ails you. Deep thought and possibly the counsel of others may be needed to surface the underlying issues.

I like to believe I have it all together, but when I mess up, the first thing I do is react to find blame in others without accepting full responsibility. This happened recently when I forgot to check my schedule and was late for an early patient at the office. I snapped at the messenger, of course, for not getting me the message earlier, my spouse who was trying to help speed my departure, and my staff, who were only trying to accommodate the patient. A problem became a mess!

After five decades on the planet, shouldn't I have learned this by now? Apparently I have not yet. But a closer look revealed this is my pattern for many little things and big things that have happened in my life and led to a recent viral illness that had perplexed me. When I do things I later regret, I blame others instead of going through the process of forgiveness. Unfortunately, over the years I trained others to take care of me in a codependent way that disempowered me and allowed them to be burdened by a burdensome nurturing role in my life.

Give thanks. Finally, I got this! Now with this awareness, I can let go of blaming and complaining and woman up! I've got my big girl panties on, finally. As more and more of this is revealed to me, I have to give thanks for the awareness and the new opportunity to choose a new way of being, responsible and upright. I am coming into alignment with my value to be accountable.

Giving love to myself and others in the circumstance of forgiveness is the next step of atonement. An apology is in order to let others know you value them and see the error of your ways. Compassion requires us to put ourselves in the other person's shoes and see how our behavior has impacted others. "Oh! What a tangled web we weave when first we practice to deceive"[6] ourselves and involve others.

I started by forgiving myself. I made a mistake. It happens. I was embarrassed. I was neglectful of my responsibilities. I apparently valued my time more than my patients by assuming my schedule was as usual instead of checking to make sure. I also devalued staff who came in early on my and the patients behalf. I was not practicing what I preach of being mindful.

I then explained and apologized to the patient. I needed to forgive myself and get her forgiveness to be in a place of service to her for her appointment. When I overreacted and was disrespectful to my coworker, she was gracious and did not disrespect or correct me. I was

6 Sir Walter Scott, in Canto VI, Stanza 17 of "Marmion" (1808), an epic poem about the Battle of Flodden Field in 1513.

out of line and she was the bigger women, a person decades my junior. I told her how much I appreciated her respect of me and how much I regretted disrespecting her in that way and asked her forgiveness. I also apologized to all my staff and the other staff that witnessed my bad behavior. I lost it, and they know I know and am accountable for doing it this time, and in the future if I do it again.

Hopefully I'll catch myself next time. There will be a next time. We are creatures of habit. But with this new awareness, I'll catch myself earlier and earlier. They know I am on notice to catch myself and they have the right to remind me if I forget. I hope to grow past this in this lifetime, hopefully soon!

Giving back is the final step. We must serve others by sharing our lessons. I am in writing this book, trying to share the lessons I've learned to move myself forward, as an example. We learn from good examples, and we learn from bad examples. The mothers in this book share plenty of both for me and hopefully for you as we all journey through the lessons of this life that bring us closer and closer to our true spiritual selves. It always comes back to our insecurities and how inadequate we feel about ourselves. I can own my mistakes unashamedly as we all make them and I'm only human. The saying, "Nobody is perfect" may be incorrect. Maybe our imperfections make us "perfectly" human.

My aunt Pearlie is my inspiration for my answer to the question, "How are you?" and I reply, "Absolutely fabulous!" I manage to feel that most of the time. When I don't feel that way, I fake it until I make it. It won't take long before I begin to focus on gratitude. Complaints are faded by the brightness of the blessings.

My aunt Pearlie enjoyed coming to the United States from Jamaica because she saw warmth among African Americans showing love, bonding, and affection. She admired the closeness, hugs, and smiles and the acknowledgment with any eye contact with just a simple nod of the head and a smile, even if not close enough for a formal greeting. In Jamaica, the West Indians had picked up the cold, distant relationships of the British colonialists. She fears this sense of community is being lost in our younger generations. She has two sons, seven grandchildren, and ten great-grands and no great-great grands yet.

Jamaicans often laugh about having so many jobs. They are full of desire to better themselves and their families. Material wealth is important, but giving and contribution to the society is even more important, so we can all receive the benefit. She has reaped the rewards working for what she has worked for and appreciating what she has been given. At this point in her life, she says, "I like being old—no responsibilities!"

There are youth who would envy the strength, clarity, peace, and vitality of my ninety-six-year-old Doctor Mom Aunt Pearlie.

My life mission, "heal and be healed," came to me in prayer. It often happens that each illness itself is a call to the healing work. I have layers of brokenness and a lot of work to do. With each layer, like peeling an onion, there are tears to shed. The healing lays upon the healed the mandate and responsibility to share with others the "good news" and in turn become a healer.

I pray to be a light of hope, encouragement, and enthusiasm in the life of others and to use my Mothers' Council to do that for my healing of myself. I pray to open myself for the spiritual messages that can illuminate the obvious in my life and the lives of my patients that are hidden right under our noses. I want to be optimistic and put a positive spin on the "good news" I need to share that can be a harsh reality of a hard lesson. I want to be the cheerleader while delivering a wakeup call.

Chapter 4

MOTHER SISTER

MOTHER SISTER IS AN OLDER sister closer to our age. Biologically she cannot be our mother, but she has contemporary experience to share with her younger sister. She is old enough to have some authority but not so much older that we do not share a lot in common. It helps that she is current and comes from a similar perspective. As we get older together, this remains a valued viewpoint to share. We learn from her triumphs as much as we learn from her blunders. She is ahead of us and can show us our next step. She is our confidant, and we can share our sister secrets.

> When your sister is your hairdresser, you need no mirror.
>
> —African proverb

This mother is our soul sister. She is extremely caring and acts as a caregiver rather than a receiver. This allows for the development of a sacred friendship. There is a willingness to care with no sense of obligation. There is no expectation. She is capable of taking care of us and showing us how to take care of ourselves and others while not being consumed in the process. She is able to receive this by giving. She gives us the attention we need to feel secure.

Mother Sister inspires us to give back the love we receive. She shows us how to *be* with others. She pampers herself and makes sure we are pampered. She knows how to work, and she knows how to play. She is creative and brings out our creativity. There is the time to work hard and there is time to have fun, and she knows how and when to do both!

She is the example of social connection. She embodies peace and beauty through patience, modesty, and courtesy. She is polite, always knowing the appropriate manners for each circumstance. As any elder would say, "She has good home training!" To her mate, she is a complement. Theirs is a sacred partnership. To her friends, she is a comrade, ally, and kindred spirit. To her peers, she is a sea of solitude. She is responsible for her actions and remains responsive to how her thoughts, words, and deeds affect her relationship with others. She exhibits joy and expresses gratitude and appreciation.

Anne Sullivan with Helen Keller

Anne Sullivan

> We have no firm hold on any knowledge or philosophy that can lift us out of our difficulties.
>
> —Anne Sullivan

Anne was the daughter of immigrant parents who came to the United States due to the great famine. She contracted an eye disease at five years old that caused repeated painful infections and scarring that led to blindness.

> It's a great mistake, I think, to put children off with falsehoods and nonsense, when their growing powers of observation and discrimination excite in them a desire to know about things.
>
> —Anne Sullivan

When she was eight years old, she ended up in an almshouse for the poor. She and her younger brother were abandoned by her father after her mother died. She felt a deep loss when her brother died within three months due to the deplorable conditions. She had the chance to undergo several eye operations with some limited short-term relief. She seized an opportunity to speak to an investigator of the home to make her case to go to a school for the blind.

> A strenuous effort must be made to train young people to think for themselves and take independent charge of their lives.
>
> —Anne Sullivan.

At Perkins School for the Blind, most of the students were from well-to-do families. Anne, fourteen when she arrived, was unable to read or write. Many students mocked her, and some teachers were irritated and impatient. As a very intelligent girl and diligent student, Anne caught up on her academic skills in a couple of years.

> Children require guidance and sympathy far more than instruction.
>
> —Anne Sullivan

A house mother, Sophia Hopkins, became her surrogate mother. Anne spent time during school vacation in her Cape Cod home. Another eye surgery improved her vision dramatically, and she was able to see well enough to read newsprint. Another mentor was Laura Bridgman, the first deaf and blind student to learn language at the school. She had been a resident for the last fifty years. Anne learned the manual alphabet from her so they were able to talk, and she would also read to her. This grandmother figure was very demanding, but Anne had a lot of patience with her. They shared a comradery as outcasts from the larger community at the school.

> Keep on beginning and failing. Each time you fail, start all over again, and you will grow stronger until you have accomplished a purpose—not the one you began with perhaps, but one you'll be glad to remember.
>
> —Anne Sullivan

Never daunted, although frequently humiliated by her struggles, she was able to excel dramatically but never conformed. She frequently broke the rules. She had a quick temper and a quick wit with a sharp tongue. She was almost expelled several times. The director at Perkins School had admired Anne Sullivan's determination, intelligence, commitment, and hard work. Her supporters helped keep her in school. In her graduation valedictorian address, she charged herself and her fellow students to live a passionate, positive, active, and earnest life and find their special part in the world.

> We can educate ourselves; we can, by thought and perseverance, develop all the powers and capacities entrusted to us, and build for ourselves true and noble characters. Because we can, we must. It is a duty we owe to ourselves, to our country and to God.
>
> —Anne Sullivan

She had to live those words willingly and faithfully when she agreed to be assigned as the teacher for seven-year-old Helen Keller, who had been deaf and blind since nineteen months. Initially a bit intimidated by such a challenge, she studied the reports of Laura Bridgman's education from her teachers. She set out to Alabama to fulfill her destiny.

> I need a teacher quite as much as Helen. I know the education of this child will be the distinguishing event of my life, if I have the brains and perseverance to accomplish it.
>
> —Anne Sullivan

> People seldom see the halting and painful steps by which the most insignificant success is achieved.
>
> —Anne Sullivan

What started out as a tumultuous relationship became the story of legend. Helen resisted Anne's teachings and her discipline. She quickly realized that she would have to abandon the strict formal method used for Laura's education. The rigid routine was stifling

Helen's progress. She knew she had to make a change. In letters to Mrs. Hopkins, Anne discussed the reasons for changing her approach.

> I am convinced that the time spent by the teacher in digging out of the child what she has put into him, for the sake of satisfying herself that it has taken root, is so much time thrown away. It's much better, I think, to assume the child is doing his part, and that the seed you have sown will bear fruit in due time. It's only fair to the child, anyhow, and it saves you unnecessary trouble.
>
> —Anne Sullivan

> I cannot explain it; but when difficulties arise, I am not perplexed or doubtful. I know how to meet them.
>
> —Anne Sullivan

She updated her plan to accommodate her active and curious student. It took an emotional toll before the breakthrough was made. It had been a test of the wills. Helen's birth mother was very indulgent of her, possibly feeling guilty about her disabilities. For Anne there was no room for pity, and with her new creative approach combined with her disciplined requirement for Helen to use proper manners, an emotional test of the wills brought about the enlightenment. Her efforts finally bore fruit when Helen realized the finger game was language. The test of their wills was over, and Helen was hungry for knowledge.

> My heart is singing for joy this morning! A miracle has happened! The light of understanding has shone upon my little pupil's mind, and behold, all things are changed!
>
> —Anne Sullivan

Helen was absorbing knowledge and information as fast as Anne could teach her. In six months she had learned 575 words, multiplication tables to five, and the Braille system—a remarkable feat for an intuitive and creative teacher as well as an eager student. Anne still relied on her mentors at the Perkins school for support and advice, but when faced with the limitations of homeschooling, she decided it would be best for them to continue her education at the Perkins School for the Blind.

> Education in the light of present-day knowledge and need calls for some spirited and creative innovations both in the substance and the purpose of current pedagogy.
>
> —Anne Sullivan

Anne Sullivan's tumultuous relationship at the Perkins school continued as she was there teaching Helen. The strained relationship was severed years later, but Anne never returned to the Perkins campus. She did stay unofficially connected through the many friendships she maintained there. Later after Anne's death, Helen returned in 1956 to the dedication for the deaf blind program's Keller-Sullivan Cottage. Anne Sullivan's methods became the centerpiece of the educational program for the deaf blind at Perkins, where she was greatly admired and deeply respected as an innovative and inspirational teacher.

> The immediate future is going to be tragic for all of us unless we find a way of making the vast educational resources of this country serve the true purpose of education, truth and justice.
>
> —Anne Sullivan

What an inspiration to us Anne Sullivan is as we continue to struggle with the inequality of the educational system, political system, and social justice system, not only in the United States but globally. We still have a lot work to do.

Yvonne

Yvonne

The woman I've become would never have unfolded the way it has without my Mother Sister Yvonne—my big sister. Mother Sister is our safety net. She is so close to us. We can identify with her and trust her. She is our sounding board.

The Oldest Girl Child

Yvonne was the second of four children and the oldest girl. My father had immigrated to the United States to find work and make a way for his family to get educated. There were many barriers to higher education in Jamaica at the time. She was born in Jamaica while he was in the United States. He didn't meet his daughter Yvonne until she was one year and three months old, when my mother arrived in the United States from Jamaica two years later with her and my two-year-old brother in tow.

Yvonne was the boss. My mother made her in charge of us younger siblings, me and my sister Carol. She became the boss of us at the very young age of nine years old. We were six and three years her junior. My sister Yvonne, not trying to get into any trouble, had a strict discipline. She could cut you like a knife with her eyes. One look could stop you dead in your tracks! If the look didn't stop us, her claw grip, arm squeezes with fingernails, and twisting pinches definitely would. She kept us in line, because if she didn't, she would have to reap the consequences for us all. It worked. She never "got it" because of us, because we had already "got it" from her!

My sister was the sacrificial lamb for the girls in our family. My brother, being the only boy child, was held to a different standard by my parents and society at large at that time. In elementary school, we all went to private Catholic school, but there was no Catholic high school in Painesville at the time, so my brother went to Cathedral Latin in Cleveland thirty miles from home. My sister was the first in a public high school and the first girl to experience dating in this country.

Head to Head with the Homeroom Advisor

The whole point of our parents' immigration to the United States was so all of us children could go to college. That was expected of all of us and known to us from a young age. We were told we could be anything we wanted to be, and my parents encouraged excellence and education. My sister Yvonne, having completed all her requirements for college, was taking vocational courses her senior year at a floral shop. A natural artist, she flourished in the position, so when she went to her Homeroom Advisor to get ready for her college applications, he discouraged her. He said she should be satisfied with her vocational training. He felt our parents didn't need to waste money on her for college. They needed to spend their money on their son, not waste it on a girl. He told her she'd get married and waste her education. Oh, no he didn't!

It was our family's daily tradition to discuss what happened at school that day at the dinner table each night at 6:00 p.m. on the dot. This night was no exception, but the news was not good. It was time for my oldest sister to prepare for college, and the homeroom advisor not only was not helpful but also discouraging.

But my sister Yvonne wanted to be a teacher, not stay working at a Floral Shop. Undone, my father, who never missed work, took off of work the next day to take care of this misunderstanding. After all, he had left his pregnant young bride in Jamaica with his infant son and came up to the United States for two years to make a new life for his family specifically so they could have opportunity for a college education, and some homeroom advisor was trying to put a kibosh on the decades-long plan. He was not having that!

Nobody knows what my father said to the administrators that day. No one in our family was ever told exactly what occurred at that meeting. My father was a reserved, articulate, and dignified man with an authoritative presence. His point was made. It was a day that changed how our family was treated in Painesville for the rest of our time in the school system. They never wanted to have to call Mr. Bernal with any bad news about his children.

Needless to say, my sister Yvonne did go to college. She became a teacher and came back to Painesville for two years to teach in the very school system that had discouraged her matriculation. I always imagined her sitting across from that homeroom advisor in a teachers' meeting, giving him a glaring "I guess I showed you" look. She was the first in our family to finish college, even though my brother was a year her senior. She went on to win awards for her teaching innovations and dedication, continuing on to get her master's and doctorate, advancing into administration, and retiring as an elementary school principal, and she has gone on to teach teachers at the university level.

Little Sisters Weekends

I was six years her junior. Her experience blazing the trail opened doors for my future. I was a junior in high school, and I wanted to go to Howard University in Washington, DC, the mecca of black education. My plan was to do well academically to get a college scholarship, but it was my Mother Sister Yvonne who helped me with college and scholarship applications. And when I had to do essays, she was my editor and spelling and grammar check before the age of computers. Heck, for years she would correct my letters I wrote to her, and she'd mail them back to me with red ink marks all over!

I think she's still tempted to do it to this day, but she gave up on me long ago. And yes, I still do like snail mail.

Little Sisters Weekends primed the pump of my already wet appetite for a college education. Visiting my sister Yvonne at Kent State University was thrilling. With the live music concerts and parties, college life looked even better than I had imagined. It was the late '60s, and the smell of reefer was in the air on campus. I got my first contact high. She knows how to laugh, play, and tease but also how to be serious and get things done. She counseled me to have fun through my college experience, but study hard, get good grades, and be humble when I pledged into our sorority. She knew I was an obnoxious teenager. Her advice worked for me. Both my sisters and I are sorority sisters. My line name was Humble Mumble. After forty years, my line sisters still call me Humble. I don't mind. I like it. I try to be it!

I got a lot of acceptances to colleges and scholarship offers being a national merit scholar during a time of affirmative action, but it was my Mother Sister Yvonne's help that secured me my full ride to my dream school. I was lucky she had come home to teach those first years. Her experience and information were more valuable than any guidance counselor. I was blessed to have her watchful guidance.

It was my sister Yvonne, not my mother, who explained everything to me about the facts of life and my menstrual cycle. I was third in line to have been given the book *Growing Up and Liking It* to explain my emerging womanhood. My mother was silent on the matter and let my sister explain everything. Yvonne also took me to the doctor to get birth control pills before I left for college.

The Big O

My father was known in the community as "the Big O." He was strict, and if a friend did not behave appropriately or used any inappropriate language, they were banished from our home. They were so intimidated by my father's expulsions that decades later as adults, friends desirous of visiting us at our parental home while we were home for the holidays called ahead to request the ban to be lifted.

It was surprising we even had dates in Painesville, because if you brought home a Bernal girl late, you were met in the driveway by my dad. Three beautiful daughters kept him up and pacing when we were out. Gentlemen callers had to come meet my parents, my father in particularly, prior to considering their potential for the date. After the nervous introductions, all dates were made aware of the curfew prior to leaving. It was a small town, so everyone knew who the suitor's people were and his reputation in the community. Not surprisingly for the times, there was no such scrutiny for the girls my brother was dating. I guess my dad felt that was the girl's dad's job! Baptized by fire, Yvonne took the worst of my father's overprotection and obsession with our dating.

The Boss

Yvonne had moved to Atlanta after the years in Painesville teaching. Active in our sorority, she has remained dedicated to public service. A devoted church member and organizer, she has served her church community in multiple capacities over the years. She has a wealth of friends and will bend over backward to help others, attracting deep and lasting friendships. Trustworthy, she is a leader of her crew. She is knowledgeable, fun loving, and creative, with a passion for her artistry as a quilt artist. She strives for excellence and is studious and meticulous with her work. Harsh and critical at times, she can be equally as complimentary. With a voluptuous figure, she has a robust social life. As a crafty person, she enjoys parties, cooking, entertaining, and having fun. No matter the social engagement, it is a creative endeavor. At a baby or bridal shower, high tea, or a quilting event there is never a dull moment. Family is important to her, and she uses her craft skills as the archivist for our family.

Our parents moved to Atlanta near my sister Yvonne when the harsh Chicago winters were wearing on them. Our parents spent years healthy and active. Our father had converted to Jehovah's Witness, and our mother began worshiping at my sister's Catholic church. They were both very active in their respective worship communities and had active lives. They had celebrated their fiftieth wedding anniversary at my sister Yvonne's home.

Our father had not been ill before the surgery. Although the surgery was a success, they lost the patient a week later. They returned to the hospital, and within hours he transitioned. He was bleeding and refused a blood transfusion. She was the executor of the estate and in charge of all the arrangements. She had no time to grieve. She had things to do, calls to make, people to inform, and there were arrangements to be made—a funeral in her father's Jehovah's Witness tradition as well a memorial in our mother's Catholic tradition. Family members came in from out of town, and there were newspapers to notify, programs and obituaries to write. She had to be strong for our mother. After fifty-one years of marriage, our mother knew of no other life. She went from her parents' home to her marriage. Mom had four children to help her, but this daughter was not the oldest but the oldest girl, and now she was in charge of making a smooth transition in the family for her father.

The memorial service was to fulfill our needs for our mourning his passing. My brother got to bare his soul speaking at the memorial. She kept it together for us so we could be free to express our grief. I completely lost it as my favorite gospel song was sung by the soloist from my sister's choir, "His eye is on the sparrow, and I know he watches me!" I was wailing, crying, and slobbering with grief, not over losing my father, since I was confident he was in ecstasy. I was in grief over my distress with my rambunctious, rebellious teenage son's fury. He had unleashed this during the repass from the funeral two days before. She had handled that situation too. She took control. She was the bossy sister. Yvonne handled things, like she always has. And now at the memorial she kept her cool. She got me water to drink and soothed me from my misery.

Yvonne is a Martha Stewart type of perfectionist who pays attention to the details. She spent hours cradling her phone and pointing out who needed to do what, when, and how. Like a dutiful caregiver, she made sure everyone else was taken care of, picked up on time, fed, and rested. She passed out exhausted at night instead of just going to sleep. She ignored her own needs, except for some reason she was having pain in her right index finger. It ached, and she could not stop it from hurting. That finger started to seize up and cramp in pain. Muscles were tight and tender. Massaging and massaging only brought temporary relief. I made the diagnosis—bossy finger! What was going on with that bossy finger?

Bossy Finger

The index finger pointing outside of us affects the world around us. My Mother Sister Yvonne needed to point that finger back at herself to see what was going on inside. There is time and circumstance to be the boss, but we all need nurturing and care as well. She needed her own time to grieve, rest, and heal. Luckily, I was able to stay with our mother for the next ten days of the transition. I was planning to be there to help with my dad's recuperation after surgery. Our mother decided, after touring several local options, not to move into a retirement village. Mom chose, for the first time, to live alone. I helped her donate our father's clothes and reorganize her closets. Yvonne still had all the legal work to hash out, but I was happy to give my Mother Sister a little break to be taken care of for a change.

A Beloved Member of Her Community

Mother Sister Yvonne has none of her own biological children but raised me and my sister, all her students and teachers, and a whole community. She cared for my elderly mother struggling with Alzheimer's disease with the love and patience of any wonderful mother. We are blessed to have had our mother there in the love, caring, and devotion of our Sister Yvonne. She is a beloved member of her community. We can't go anywhere in Atlanta without running into some friend, parent, teacher, or student anxious to greet my Mother Sister Yvonne.

I Let the Universe Channel Creative Energy through Me

Mother Sister is all about creativity. She wants to leave the world a more benevolent and beautiful place than when she arrived. It is no surprise that these two Mother Sisters were both creative educators dedicated to uplifting society. Mother Sister reminds us that we are here to create. She uses her creative power to make sure we are empowered to be all we can be, in line with the creative power of the universe.

Chapter 5

Mother Wit

Mother Wit is a trickster. In a deck of cards, she would be the Joker or the Wild Card. We never know what she will come up with next, but we realize she will get to the heart of the matter. She brings our sensitive issues to the surface. She helps us with denial. She is a master of illusion herself, and therefore she can see through our disguises.

Often our young adolescent preparing for young womanhood brings the gift of Mother Wit. This gift can be stifled by adults who feel it is inappropriate. It can be rude and disrespectful if it is used for back talking elders. But often it is with humor and clarity of the child's deep inner knowing. It should be cultivated, not extinguished. It can be their way of bringing complicated emotion into the light. With openness and care, this type of sharing can lead to problem solving within our family and community relationships. It can also, when used constructively, build character and confidence.

The gift of wit was celebrated in my household growing up. We would often play clever word games, especially at Sunday dinners. Bantering back and forth, we would get two points for a witty retort and a three-point play if we were particularly savvy! But this took a bad turn in my adolescence when I became sassy, especially with my mother. I was the baby of the family. I guess my mother was tired after my three older siblings, and I did not get the wrath she would have raised against them. I was a smart aleck! I would take it to the point of disrespect by rolling my eyes and sucking my teeth. In my day and time, that was tantamount to blasphemy! It has taken years to temper my sarcastic nature. Now I use the gift of humor to bring sensitive truths to the surface in my doctor-patient relationships.

Fa Mulan

Fa Mulan

Fa Mulan is my Mother Wit because she is a master of illusion. She was able to challenge the status quo of her time by tricking the authorities with her service in the armed forces instead of her elderly father or young brothers. It would not have been righteous for any of these family members to serve at that time. She was at a crossroads. She saw a path that others would not have even considered. Therefore, despite the risk to her own life, she devised a way to protect them and bring honor to her family.

Disney took many liberties in writing the story of this ancient historical figure, Fa Mulan. She was the teenage daughter of a general who had no sons of age to go to war for the family. Her father was injured and infirmed. She decided to disguise herself as a man and go in his place. But she was hardly the naive young girlie girl portrayed in the animated feature. She was a powerfully trained woman warrior, well-schooled and skilled in martial arts. She was a skilled horsemen and archer. She had physical prowess even prior to substituting herself for her father's position in the war.

She is my Mother Wit because she was successful at achieving war hero status and never being found out to be a woman during her twelve-year tenure in the military service. She fought in many bloody campaigns. She was so skilled in battle that she had moved up twelve ranks. Her notoriety and acumen afforded her the opportunity to be assigned to the imperial council. She was offered and did refuse that position, choosing to accept a fine horse instead. She returned home and resumed her quiet life and true female identity with her family. There is no record of a love affair between her and her supervising officer. It was only then when her military comrades visited her home after the war that they learned of her true female identity.

I am in awe of this Mother Wit who was able to fool her comrades and superiors while serving so heroically. On a practical level, she had to hide her female physical differences, her elimination, her monthly cycle, and her feminine attributes and masquerade male attributes in mannerisms and voice and mimicking growing facial hair. On a mental level she could have never let her guard down. She must have slept with one eye open! She had to be clever to know what to say and how to say it. On an emotional level, she had to mimic the masculinity of her time. I expect it was not much different from the virile, testosterone-fueled, smug, arrogant boldness of the young male warriors of today. But not only did she conceal her gender, but she also excelled as a male warrior moving up the ranks swiftly. On a spiritual level, she honored and protected her family. But had she gotten caught, it would have been a disgrace. This Mother Wit would never let that happen. She was on a mission. She got the job done!

This Mother Wit used deception for a noble purpose. Often we use masks because we are clouded by self-judgment. Mother Wit knows that most of us are ruled by our perceptions and conditioning. This mother realizes that our freedom lies in our ability to evaluate and control our thoughts and actions. She understands that every thought is a crossroads for a determination of our beliefs and our behaviors. Mother Wit makes us realize we actually have those choices to make over and over again throughout our day. Most of us defer to our conditioned responses and wonder why we keep getting the same situations we have experienced in the past. We are unconsciously recreating them again and again. Mother Wit brings this to our consciousness with her penetrating gaze, crumbling the façade of our illusion.

Mother Wit meets us at the crossroads to lead us to discovery and enlightenment. She helps us identify the enemy within ourselves that leaves us open to attack. She causes us to challenge our habitual ways of thinking and believing by showing ourselves to us in the mirror. She does it bluntly and brashly, never mincing words. She is a prankster but with definite focus. She leads us to the discovery of the error of our ways. With her insight, we can choose the road to our recovery. We are directed by the transparency she brings. When we have rid ourselves of the enemy inside of us, the enemy outside of us cannot stand, and we do not have to defend against the attack.

When I was going through the struggles of my first marriage, I was at a crossroads. I was trying to decide my next strategy to "fix" my marriage. I told my husband my plans to be silent for the weekend. Our children would be away with friends, and I would be in silence after work on Friday. He was drinking again and took the opportunity that Friday evening to taunt me. Spitefully at one point he blurted out, "You were nothing until you married me!" I never spoke. It never resonated in one fiber of being. I am blessed to know my connection with the creator of the universe and all humanity. I never responded. Sadly, I wondered, was that a projection of his feeling about himself? Ultimately, he did apologize for that statement. He was intending to be hurtful, but I knew it was because he was hurting.

Weekend of Silence

I ended up leaving for that weekend. I retreated to Earth Mother Sabrina's home for silent meditation while she was out of town. My marriage was failing, and I felt a lot of guilt. I had taken my marital vows before friends and family. I had expected our marriage to last a lifetime, until death do us part. Marriage counseling had not lasted long. When he refused to get the help for his alcoholism, he stopped showing up to the sessions. Different counselors, different priests, all came to the same dead end. I was working with Al-anon for six years and embracing the twelve steps. I was codependent no more! I prayed for answers. I walked in the natural beauty of the surroundings. I breathed, I prayed, I did yoga, and I meditated. I was looking for the void. I was seeking the silent stillness of my mind.

I had a dream. My husband and I were on a theater stage tied together.

In the audience were the people, friends, and family who attended our wedding fifteen years earlier. In addition, there were marriage encounter and spiritual retreat participants, our church family, societal circle members, and family friends we had gathered over the years. These were the witnesses of our union and our vows. A master of ceremonies appeared, and it was our priest. He began the eulogy of our marriage. At the end, he untied the knot and we were free.

Wedding Funeral

I had heard of rituals that Native American cultures performed to end a marital journey. In my dream state, I had experienced a wedding funeral. I awakened clear. I had no regrets and no guilt. The message I was asking for, I received: Get a lawyer!

Internal Change

Mother Wit challenges us. She can act as our mirror reflecting our own issues back to us. Her light can clarify the confusion of the experiences that have wounded us. Were we ignored or neglected as children? Were we smothered and overprotected, not allowed to express ourselves? Were we pushed to do things we never desired to do? Mother Wit is blunt yet logical. She is profoundly honest and frank. Her words have a sharp edge that can cut deep. She highlights when we are unconsciously projecting our own feelings onto others, passing on our pain, fears, and negativity. She spotlights our projecting our hopes and dreams on others, especially onto our children. Mother Wit helps us focus on moral issues within our society, our family, as well as within the self.

Alake

Alake

She was a street-wise woman, born 1939 in Memphis, Tennessee. Her words were short by provocative, brief but clear, and she was a quick study of academics and of people. She enjoyed a close relationship with her aunt and uncle growing up. She graduated high school in 1956 but earned her BS degree in 1982.

> We who believe in freedom cannot rest. We who believe in freedom cannot rest until it comes.
>
> —"Ella's Song" by Dr. Bernice Johnson Reagon

She had earlier pursued a career as a biochemist, but concerned with human rights and injustices perpetrated against people of color, she pursued a law degree. In her legal practice, she focused on prisoners' rights, criminal appeals, and bankruptcy. She was an uncompromising advocate for the political, social, spiritual, and cultural agenda of African people, using her knowledge of the law for her people's liberation. She had an acceptance of the difference in the legal system working for people of color and devised alternative strategies to mitigate the biases. Going to court, she was always prepared within the legal realm with additional preparation and protection within the spiritual realm. She was very committed to African people and advocating for people coming from other countries, and she also practiced immigration law.

She was practical and didn't believe in wasting your time or hers. Even in a situation of injustice, she knew when to cut her losses and move forward. When one of our circle sisters was having trouble with a car insurance company that had continued to take her money, defaulted without informing her, and did not provide her coverage,

Alake advised her to count her blessings. During all that time, she hadn't had any accidents, needed the coverage, or gotten stopped by the police. Though it was unjust, unfair, and illegal, the expense of litigation wasn't worth the time, mental energy, and money. She advised her to look at the money spent as an offering to the universe that protected her and that the people responsible would pay. There is no escape from divine law! This gave her comfort. Our sister was able to move on.

> Emancipate yourselves from mental slavery; none but ourselves can free our mind.
>
> —Bob Marley from "Redemption Song"

She embraced a pan-African philosophy in lifestyle, culture, attitude, and action. She legally changed her name at that time to embrace her African cultural heritage. She was a founder of the Elders Council of Washington, DC, and member and advisor to the republic of New Africa and many local, national, and international diasporic causes. She practiced West African Yoruba faith and in 2003 fulfilled a dream to return to her Nigerian homeland.

An Advocate for Her Grandchildren

She understood the preeminence of family. She has lived true to her beliefs, respecting her natal family but not being ruled by their path in choosing her own future. A vigilant advocate for her people but an unbelievable advocate for her grandchildren, this Mother Wit became the primary caretaker for her grandson. She was also intimately involved in assisting with her two granddaughters. She wanted them to feel a part of the family. She wanted her grandchildren to have an African-centered education to connect to their heritage and understand their own personal self-worth. Education was important to her. She guided and tutored her grandchildren. She was an actively involved grandparent at their school.

Consequence is no coincidence.

—from "Lost Ones" by Lauryn Hill

I came to know Alake from our woman's circle. We worked with rite-of-passage programs for adolescents and all age groups of members as well. A yearly activity involves a heart-to-heart sharing for support by our circle sisters. She delighted in this sharing, appreciating the camaraderie of like-minded women. She spoke in simple terms, blunt and unfiltered. Nothing was sugar-coated. Not a woman of many words, she kept things brief and to the point. She was outspoken, and her comments could smack you in the face. But she always had something very culminating to contribute.

Inquiring Minds Want to Know

She was a keen listener and always trying to look at things from a different angle, from a new and interesting point of view and alternative frame of reference that you may have not considered. Her observations could be a bitter pill to swallow. Mama Alake was an inquirer. She asked us questions until we discovered our own truth. This Mother Wit challenged us to challenge ourselves and our beliefs and to question our true values—not what we say we value but what we show we value by our actions and priorities. Were we following an expected path but not considering and questioning everything? Were we open to new ideas? Her questioning allowed us to examine ourselves intensely for inconsistencies? Her inquiry was probing, focused, and piercing, getting to the underlying essence of things, making it clear and cutting to the chase. I'm glad I was never her opponent. I'm glad she was always looking out for us.

One particular year I had quite a long discussion in the circle. I was troubled by my teenage son. He had been struggling since my divorce from his dad, and now I had a new mate. We had been secretly preparing for marriage for the past eight months. We hesitated to announce a formal engagement until things settled down with my son.

It had been tumultuous. My son was having a difficult time and acting out of anger and uncertainty. His high school attendance officer and I were on a first-name basis. The men from his rite-of-passage program convened at my home to try to assist us during this difficult time of family transition and defuse tension, as we had one crisis after another. Over the last two and a half years, we were seen by psychiatrists, phycologists, social workers, priests, laymen, and school councilors from three separate high schools. I had never wanted him to leave our home after the divorce. But he decided to go live with his father. My lawyer advised me to honor my son's wishes, because he was at the age where he could choose. Luckily, it was not long before he wanted to come back home to live with me again. We tried at-risk programs, live-in halfway houses, public and private interventions. He resented me for this, but I didn't know what else to do at the time. My father died unexpectedly a few months later. My son, daughter, and I immediately left for Atlanta for my father's funeral.

When my boyfriend came to support me in Atlanta, my son felt blindsided by my boyfriend's arrival. My son exploded again out of anger, uncertainty, and betrayal. He didn't want my boyfriend there. He was not taking the divorce well. My son had admitted to me later that he expected his father to "get himself together" and that his father and I would be remarried. It was all just too much! I wept, I grieved, and I broke down during my dad's memorial service. It was not for my Father—he had gone to glory—but for the turmoil of my life. Lost and confused, I didn't know what to do. I had just returned from the funeral a couple of weeks before our meeting. Looking for help and guidance, I bared my soul to my sisters.

> You think you're in charge! We ain't in charge!
>
> —Mama Alake

Alake listened attentively. I knew divorced women who believe that women should not remarry until their children are out of the house. My daughter was five years old at the time. Thirteen years as a vibrant women single and alone didn't seem to be right to me. "Why do you care what other women think?" she inquired. I began to look inside myself. Her piercing inquiries let me realize I was judging myself a failure for having to get a divorce in the first place. I was looking outside myself for validation and maybe even a form of punishment for my mistake. Like I didn't deserve happiness. "You believe that?" she asked with a piercing gaze. "No, it's nonsense!" I answered.

The penetrating inquiry of this Mother Wit brought me to my truth. Her blunt, out of the mouth, and often sarcastic probing allowed me to focus and get to the underlying essence of my thoughts and feelings. Talking of my challenges with my son and how this affected my relationship with him and my new mate, she remarked, "There goes your energy. You're giving it away!" All of a sudden, it was obvious. My mind opened. "You think you are in charge. We ain't in charge!" she said. Through the haze of guilt, fear, and shame lifting, I became focused and clear.

What Alake taught me was surrender. I have the responsibility for my intention, my efforts, my emotions, my thoughts and actions, and my role in relating to others. But the insight and understanding come into play in that those things are only a part of the outcome. I am not in control of that, nor should I be. Life is a prayer of co-creation. It is the mystery and discovery of how the all flows from the individual parts. We are each an indivisible duality, both human and divine. How we are all interconnected at deeper and deeper levels is too profound for our minds to comprehend but not too removed for our hearts to touch, feel, and know.

She cut to the chase. "What do you want?" I smiled. "My new family! My fiancé as my husband and the father of my children or at least my young daughter. To do everything I can to help my son through the grief of losing his granddad, his family as he knew it, his family home, his previous expectations for future, and the reality of his father's new life choices and my new life choice to remarry." Then she smiled as well. "There's the passion!" she remarked.

She was a very colorful person. Her favorite response to anything that pleases her with a big smile was a robust, "Yeeeaaaahhh!" At the end of our discussion, that is what she said, and that is just how I felt! That is why Alake is my Mother Wit. Her inquiry was short but provocative, brief, but made me clear. She played the devil's advocate to provoke me to know the right thing for me by illuminating what should have been obvious.

Mother wit can be a temptress or a scoundrel. She can be both the good angel and the devil on our shoulders simultaneously. She can be a comedian or come off as harsh. Either way she tests us to become our true selves. This tested me but alerted me. But I followed my intuition, and I was not only able to escape misfortune but to find peace.

It has all turned out, as it always does, some kind of way. My new husband and I got married that December, three months later. My son announced as I walking out the door to the wedding that he was not coming. I kissed him on the cheek and let him know I'd see him after my honeymoon. He went to the Challenge Academy that winter. He graduated high school that July with honors and was awarded a partial college scholarship by that program. My son and I still faced struggles over the next few years, but we reconciled with our Earth Mother Sabrina's help and forgave each other, appreciating the lessons learned. Years later he has come to appreciate and even respect my husband, glad to have him part of the family.

> Wisdom is better than silver and gold.
>
> —from "Lost Ones" by Lauryn Hill

Self-sacrificing, Alake gave up her lucrative law practice to raise her grandson. They relocated to Atlanta. I missed her at our gatherings. Then I heard she had been ill with cancer. She transitioned in 2004. I had to chuckle when I heard she put her plans for her funeral in place, down to the songs, the singers, the obituary, and the program. She had all her legal and financial ducks in a row, just as I would have expected. Although I was not able to attend, I love the picture her daughter chose for her memorial. Eyes peering over her sunglasses, she's looking down on us now with that piercing gaze, "Keeping us honest and keeping it *real*!"

Self-Awareness

Mother Wit gives us inner vision. Sharp and witty, she made us constructively critical of ourselves. Clever with words with attention to facts, data, and details, Mother Wit helps us find our true selves. When we are stuck in reaction with our usual habitual actions, she helps illuminate for us our need to respond differently by spotlighting our own inner sight. Through her process of a rattling our cage into enlightenment, she leads us back to awaken our sleeping dreams.

Chapter 6
Lawyer Mother

Her symbol is justice. She demands truth, order, and decorum. Her expectation is respectability. Lawyer Mother is devoted to cultivating our ability to distinguish between right and wrong and to distinguish being real or fake. This is a milestone our Lawyer Mother helps us to conquer, hopefully as teenagers, during our coming of age of personal responsibility, before we are thrust into adulthood. She does this as our counselor when we have the foresight to ask her advice before we make an ill-fated decision. She does this as our advocate if we come to her after an ill-advised mistake. As she gets us out of the predicaments of our life, she guides us through to a new way of thinking that will hopefully allow us to avoid at least that predicament again!

> Be a silent man or woman, and not a hot head.
>
> —the teachings of Ptahotep

Lawyer Mother is our model for right speech, to speak truth despite fear, with courage. She makes speech her servant. She shares her wisdom. Lawyer Mother expresses herself mindfully. She understands words as a symbolic language for the purposes of communication. She knows that there is meaning beyond the words we speak by how the voice is modulated. An inflection or intonation can make all the difference. Lawyer Mother speaks with her listener in mind. She says what the listener needs to hear, rather than what she wants to say to them, in the way she wants to say it. This is the basis of the virtuous and honorable thoughts and intention of the speaker. She can speak truth, avoid deception and lies, and effectively communicate in a way that does not do any deliberate harm. She always avoids harsh words and gossip. Words have power and can injure or inspire! Her words are for enlightenment, empowerment, and inspiration.

Maya Angelou

Maya Angelou

Maya's Journey

> "I believe that each of us comes from the creator trailing wisps of glory."[7]
>
> —Maya Angelou

Maya Angelou was thought to be partially descended from the Mende people of West Africa. Her maternal great-grandmother was an emancipated slave after the civil war. Maya described her as "that poor little Black girl, physically and mentally bruised." After a legal battle for paternity from her former white slave owner, she lost the case and was sent to the poorhouse. Her daughter, Marguerite Baxter, was Angelou's grandmother. Her paternal grandmother, Annie Henderson, was a powerful figure in her life who was an entrepreneur who thrived during the great depression and World War II because she made wise and honest investments. We all, like Maya Angelou, were winners of a lotto jackpot when we are born out of a legacy of many ancestors who survived. Out of how many eggs and sperm that could come together, this egg and this sperm made Marguerite Annie Johnson, the unique soul that became known as Maya Angelou.

> "You may not control all the events that happen to you, but you can decide not to be reduced by them."
>
> —Maya Angelou-*Letter to my Daughter*, RH in letter on page xii

[7] Used with Permission of Caged Bird Legacy LLC, www.MayaAngelou.com

Out of tragedy a star was born. She was raised by her paternal grandparents after her parents' divorce. She returned to her mother's care in St. Louis, only to be raped by her mother's boarder at the age of seven and a half. She spoke the name of the perpetrator, and he was subsequently murdered. She thought she was to blame for his death. She stopped talking. She returned south to her grandmother's care and protection.

> "Nothing can dim the light which shines from within."[8]
>
> —Maya Angelou

She withdrew from family and peers in preparation for her future relationship with words and sounds. During the "silent years," she read every book in the library. It was her relationship with Ms. Flowers, a member of her community who took a special interest in her, that gave her back her voice. She inspired her by reading poetry to her, telling her that poetry is music written for the human voice and challenging her to speak those words. She had been mute for almost five years.

> "We may encounter many defeats but we must not be defeated."[9]
>
> —Maya Angelou

She pursued many quests and faced trials during her young life. She relentlessly pursued and left school to work as the first black female streetcar conductor in San Francisco. She completed high school at the age of seventeen and soon after gave birth to her son. She had a series of occupations as a young adult, including fry chef, prostitute, nightclub dancer, and performer.

---

8 ibid

9 ibid

> "Love recognizes no barriers. It jumps hurdles, leaps fences, penetrates walls to arrive at its destination full of hope."[10]
>
> —Maya Angelou

She recounts in an autobiography the story of being beaten, tortured, and held prisoner. She was rescued, vindicated, and nurtured back to health by her mother. Although her mother was not a good mother for a young child, Maya felt that she was a great mother for an adolescent, young adult, and adult. She inspired her to become all she could be.

> "You are the sum total of everything you've ever seen, heard, eaten, smelled, been told, forgot—it's all there. Everything influences each of us, and because of that I try to make sure that my experiences are positive."[11]
>
> —Maya Angelou

Both a victim and a heroine of the civil right struggle in the 1960s, she read and studied voraciously, mastering French, Spanish, Italian, Arabic, and the West African language Fanti. While in Ghana, she met with Malcolm X. In 1964, she returned to America to help him build the Organization of African American Unity. She was devastated and adrift after Malcolm X was assassinated, and the organization dissolved. Soon after his assassination, Dr. Martin Luther King Jr. asked Maya Angelou to serve as northern coordinator for the Southern Christian Leadership Conference. King's assassination, falling on her fortieth birthday in 1968, devastated her.

Phoenix Rising

Her resurrection and rebirth was articulated in her poem "Still I

[10] ibid

[11] ibid

Rise." She used her art to struggle through her depression, writing, producing, and narrating a ten-part series of documentaries on blues music and the African American heritage called *Blacks, Blues, Black*. The following year she published her first autobiography, *I Know Why the Caged Bird Sings,* which brought her international recognition and acclaim.

> "My mission in life is not merely to survive, but to thrive; and to do so with some passion, some compassion, some humor, and some style."[12]
>
> —Maya Angelou

From that point her ascension as an American author, poet, dancer, actress, singer, and film star was propelled. Spanning over fifty years, she published seven autobiographies, three books of essays, and several books of poetry and was credited with a list of plays, movies, and television shows. She received over fifty honorary degrees and dozens of awards.

Phenomenal Woman

Maya Angelou continued her work in civil rights. Dr. Angelou has served on two presidential committees. She composed and read her poem "On the Pulse of the Morning" at President Clinton's inauguration in 1993 at his request. It was broadcast live around the world. In 2000, she was awarded the Presidential Medal of Arts and received the National Medal of Arts. She delivered the poem "Amazing Peace" at the 2005 President George W. Bush Christmas tree lighting ceremony. President Barack Obama presented her the country's highest civilian honor, the Presidential Medal of Freedom, in 2010.

12 ibid

Maya's Legacy

> "The ache for home lives in all of us, the safe place where we can go as we are and not be questioned."[13]
>
> —Maya Angelou

She was a mother of one son. However, she mothered many. Her words are a living legacy for my life. The last time I saw her was in Harrisburg. When she spoke at that college auditorium to hundreds, it was like we were all sitting in her living room having a chat about her remarkable life. She was like a friend and elder member of the family. Though she left us, her words are left behind to empower. A counselor, guide, and advocate she is our Lawyer Mother. She is a life teacher who has led by example. What better role model for our adolescents and for all of us?

> "Easy reading is damned hard writing."
>
> — Nathaniel Hawthorne often quoted by Maya Angelou

She was able to weave words together. Maya's writings help with our consideration of intangible ideologies to enable us to gain an expansive vision of life's most important questions. Why do I feel this way? Why do I act this way? How can I change these patterns in my life? It was her ability to wordsmith with creativity and integrity that gave her the ability to touch our souls. Reading her words can offer a spiritual experience, and this is why she is so widely beloved and respected for her craft. This word warrior was teaching us the importance of the use of language. Words do matter. Words can change the way we feel, the things we believe, and the direction of our lives.

---

13 ibid

We will explore how Maya Angelou's words have given us perspectives on karma, self-determination, justice, bigotry, virtue, ignorance, intelligence, wisdom, jealousy, patience, complaining, forgiving, self-expression, creativity, her love of service to others, and the legacy she has left us.

> Karma: "I learned that you should not go through life with catcher's mitts on both hands; you need to be able to throw something back." [14]
>
> —Maya Angelou

In this modern era of "what have you done for me lately" consumerism, it is easy to forget that we have a responsibility to share, to give back, and to get rid of things that do not work for us. It can be hard to break away from traditions and habits. Often we are not grateful for what we have received and have taken much too much for granted. Excess could lead to arrogant expectancy, privilege, and superiority. This causes a disconnection where we do not feel a responsibility to others. However, with good home training we know "to whom much is given, much is expected." The food, clothing, and shelter provided by our parents at that time may not have been easy to provide. Others around the world do not have access to basics we in the Western world take for granted. We do not have to go to a third-world country to experience this. Often we can go into our inner city or our rural poverty areas or in our own backyards. Maya was a religious person and spread her good fortune with her charitable giving. Though generous and sharing, she remained grateful and prudent. She avoided excesses.

> Self-determination: "Nothing will work unless you do." [15]
>
> —Maya Angelou

---

[14] ibid

[15] ibid

We are in our adolescence in our coming of age of personal responsibility. Gone are the days when we are babied by our parents. It is now time for us to take more responsibility in our lives. It is time for us to start taking care of ourselves at a different level. We are starting to plan for what we are to do with our futures. We are differentiating ourselves from our parents. We are making choices and are looking outside of our families and community for a broader world view. Our character defines us. It is important to know certain Golden Rules to live by. Hopefully our parents are a good role models these. But if not, this Lawyer Mother Maya Angelou gives us food for thought we should consider.

> Justice: "It is impossible to struggle for civil rights, equal rights for blacks, without including whites. Because equal rights, fair play, Justice, are all like the air: We all have it, or none of us has it. That is the truth of it."[16]
>
> —Maya Angelou

This Lawyer Mother upholds heavenly law and order through justice, creating peace, and allowing faith, hope, and love to reign supreme on this earthly plane of existence. She had the ability to distinguish between right and wrong and to distinguish between real and unreal, natural law from man's law, and the truth from the lie agreed upon. This vision and courage is the leadership that moves a consciousness of the human race forward. If we all could share this sense of optimism, love, and peace, abundance would flow to all God's children, and our world would be a better place.

> Bigotry: "Prejudice is a burden that confuses the past, threatens the future and renders the present inaccessible."
>
> —Maya Angelou *All God's Children Need Traveling Shoes*—RH, page 155

[16] ibid

As a human rights activist, civil rights activist, and humanitarian, Maya Angelou had the courage to extricate bigots from her home, not wanting their words to pollute her environment. She had a magnanimous personality with a moral sense, and she was always striving for advancement and social welfare in a positive manner. She was law-abiding only when laws were just and fair, and she espoused philosophies that were optimistic, holistic, and dedicated to a social equilibrium.

> Virtue: "One isn't necessarily born with courage, but one is born with potential. Without courage, we cannot practice any other virtue with consistency. We can't be kind, true, merciful, generous, or honest."[17]
>
> —Maya Angelou

When we receive spiritual intuition, we are often hesitant to speak (or act) on that truth. Her life is a testament to resiliency. She was a warm, loving, open, soul-filled being with courage that she cultivated through her lifetime. She was our voice when we did not have the words to express our feelings. She expressed them for us in her writing, poetry, drama, song, and dance. She lived a life of no regrets because negative experiences had lost their power over her by her writing, sharing, and releasing.

> Ignorance: "My mother said I must always be intolerant of ignorance but understanding of illiteracy. That some people, unable to go to school, were more educated and more intelligent than college professors." [18]
>
> —Maya Angelou

---

17 ibid

18 ibid

Maya Angelou is our Lawyer Mother. She is our teacher. Do we have faith in her ability to teach us truth? She expresses her thoughts, feelings, and perception mindfully. She is our model for right speech, to speak truth, despite fear, with courage. The expression of our emotions can be reflected in the art of a culture, giving insightful soul communication. She is able to put words together, to enable others to acquire a broader view of the subjects at hand.

> Intelligence: "I'm grateful to intelligent people. That doesn't mean educated. That doesn't mean intellectual. I mean really intelligent. What black old people used to call "mother wit" means intelligence that you had in your mother's womb. That's what you rely on. You know what's right to do." [19]
>
> —Maya Angelou

We are born into this life open to divine inspiration. Childhood brings refreshing ideas, bold action, and unfiltered words led by spiritual guidance that is instinctual and natural, but not necessarily welcomed or nurtured by most of us adults. The process of socialization of modern Western society favors obedience to our parents and caregivers rather than the obedience to follow that divine guidance. The faith of most adults is concretely in the seen, our educational knowledge, and our religious doctrine, not the unseen intuitive leadership of one's spirit. Most of us remain slaves to our conditioned reactions rather than those unprompted, inspired responses. How many times have infants' or toddlers' spontaneous responses to a stranger been abruptly halted by parental biases? My own daughter picked her own godmother at her first birthday ritual, crawling into her lap and falling asleep. But did we listen to her choice that her actions requested? No, we chose another godmother who, unfortunately, has not been in her life since her father and I divorced. But later when my daughter insisted on us making her chosen godmother official, I didn't resist.

---

19 ibid

At three years old, my daughter picked out the man who would become her future stepfather. I had just divorced. I was seeking my own healing at an Iyanla Vanzant Empowerment Retreat, and my daughter was staying with family friends from our church. Their daughter was having a birthday party that weekend. Other friends and church members were there for the celebration. In the midst of that party, my daughter crawled into this man's lap to take a nap. Others, who did not know him, commented to him what a beautiful daughter he had and how she looked just like him. I knew nothing of this story until a year later when we began courting. We married the following year. He has been her "daddy" ever since, and she is his precious "daddy's girl." It is a miracle if our children get to adulthood without adults stifling their soul wisdom: that spiritual knowing through an open heart. For adults who retain it or elders who reclaim it, these are the ones who are known to possess the "Mother Wit," but it is inside us all, waiting for the miracle of our self-discovery.

> Wisdom: "A wise woman wishes to be no one's enemy;
> a wise woman refuses to be anyone's victim." [20]
>
> —Maya Angelou

One of my favorite works of Maya Angelou is *Letter to My Daughter.* It is one that I shared with my own daughter. It is full of soul wisdom. We can be arrogant and strong headed and jeopardize the success that could be gained by listening to wise counsel. We can even bullheadedly make enemies where there was no battleground. Maya Angelou's example helps us to gain insight into our life's experiences by using concepts, ideas, and thoughtful reflection she has shared on her life experiences. Living a contemplative life through abstract thinking and deep thought, her expertise was uniting the aspect of human psychology and behavior to promote wellbeing in personal endeavors and for spiritual development. She teaches us about

---

[20] ibid

ourselves and our brothers and sisters and becoming all that we are created to be.

> Jealousy: "Jealousy in romance is like salt in food. A little can enhance the savor, but too much can spoil the pleasure and, under certain circumstances, can be life-threatening."
>
> —Maya Angelou, *Wouldn't Take Nothing for My Journey Now,* page 129, Random House, New York

Often romance sparks the flame that can grow, mature, and then transform into true love. A little jealousy can keep the romance alive but insecurity is not healthy. True love, not just romance, gives us the courage to sacrifice for others due to our selfless love and devotion.

> Patience: "Little by little grows the banana."
>
> —African Congo proverb often quoted by Maya Angelou

There is a goal-setting strategy called baby steps. Often people are in a haste to get to the end without enough contemplation on the process. Moving forward puts one step in front of the other and requires a slow, steady pace to make progress. Care must be taken to follow a step-wise order to build the platform for the next step. Skipping important steps can cause the whole thing to come tumbling down. Slow and steady wins the race. Be patient. Enjoy the process. It is the majority of the journey. It is growth that takes time for the process to mature, and the culmination is when it is ripe. In our Jamaican culture, we enjoy bananas through the entire process. Boil the green banana, mash it, and eat it with salt and butter as a part of a breakfast meal. We eat the ripe banana, using it for snacks, meals, and desserts, and the overripe banana we use for banana fritters. There is much to look forward to all along the way.

> Complaining: "What you're supposed to do when you don't like a thing, change it. If you can't change it, change the way you think about it. Don't Complain."
>
> —Maya Angelou, *Wouldn't Take Nothing for My Journey Now,* RH, page 87

Complaining distracts us from seeing the potential available to us. In our haste to judgment and victimization, we embrace what is only one possibility as the truth and make it our self-fulfilling prophecy. It distracts our capacity for creative thinking and strategic planning and our ability to organize and structure a solution to the problem at hand. Complaining halts our forward motion. It stalls us dead in our tracks. Complaining is just spinning our wheels and digging a bigger hole for ourselves. Vent and then repent. After we get it off our chest, we must forgive ourselves for any negativity and move on. If we cannot change our situation, we can change our attitude about it, and at least our perspective will change.

> Forgiveness: "You can't forgive without loving. And I don't mean sentimentality. I don't mean mush. I mean having enough courage to stand up and say, "I forgive. I'm finished with it."[21]
>
> —Maya Angelou

Forgiveness is a choice of our free will to let go of negativity and embrace our true spiritual selves. It takes courage to let go of blame, shame, guilt, and regret to accept the lesson in love and move forward renewed, cleansed, and whole. It is our attachment to our emotional and ego-based conditioning that can lead to the merciless use of our free will. Holding on to hostility, anger, and feelings of revenge only comes back to pollute our own spirit with toxins, creating bad vibes. Let it go!

---

[21] ibid

> Self-expression: "A bird does not sing because it has an answer, it sings because it has a song."
>
> —Chinese proverb often quoted by Maya Angelou

There is a "song" in everyone's heart. It can be expressed in as many ways as there has been and will be lifetimes of human beings. We choose our song in the way we choose to express our life and in our legacy of being. What three words would describe the way we are "being" in this world? If we go to trusted friends, they can tell us the *tune* we are singing. If that description pleases us, we can continue the way we are being in the world, delighted at our song. This is our "heart song." It is the message from our soul's passion. It inspires us and motivates us to fly higher and higher.

If what our trusted friend tells us displeases us and is *not* our intention, we need to change our ways and choose a new way of being. This is our "ego song." It's a broken record we have heard so long or so often we are repeating it again and again. We must train ourselves to become all we are destined to be. Otherwise we can be trapped in the continuation of the perils of our past, bringing us around in circles and condemning us to the same desolate future. Honesty requires us to detach from the emotions that could be used to halt us, stagnate us, or manipulate us. Then we will not allow ourselves to be used or abused. Opening our minds, having the courage to be obedient to our open heart, reveals our soul's calling. It is up to us to answer that call. Open your heart! Your soul is calling. Answer it!

> Creativity: "I believe that each of us comes from the creator trailing wisps of glory. We come from the Creator with creativity. I think that each one of us is born with creativity."[22]
>
> —Maya Angelou

[22] ibid

Creativity is a gift of our creator, and we are made in that image, cut from the same cloth. It is humility and gratitude for our challenges that inspire us. It is gifts and talents granted to us that we share our creativity with others.

> Service: "Try to be a Rainbow in someone's cloud."
>
> —Maya Angelou, *Letter to My Daughter,* page xii

"Bad" times come to all of us as part of the cycle of life and death, sickness and health, bitter and sweet, strong and weak. Hard times come into everyone's life—our friends, neighbors, enemies, and strangers. To give or receive a smile can help us see a glimmer of light in our darkest night, a ray of sunshine on our cloudy day, or the light at the end of the tunnel. Our service to others in positivity and purpose makes any bitter pill easier to swallow, even our own.

> Legacy: "I've learned that people will forget what you said, people will forget what you did, but people will never forget how you made them feel."[23]
>
> —Maya Angelou

You only have one chance to make a positive first impression. Even if you are having a bad day, try to fake it till you make it. Do not take it out on other people. It is not their fault. Our legacy with others is in the feelings that we share. Relating with love and caring and uplifting our thoughts, words, and deeds uplifts us all. Hurtful mean-spiritedness appeals to the fearful ego part of our most base mundane nature. We decide.

Dr. Maya Angelou

This bold truth teller, Dr. Maya Angelou, helped us with our lies

[23] ibid

and shame. We lie when we are ashamed. We are out of integrity and afraid of embarrassment. We judge ourselves inadequate and judge others as lacking the compassion and understanding for the truth. This is without even giving them a chance to be that for us. This creates a barrier to intimacy. There is now a lie between us. If we are close, then they realize we are lying and have broken the bonds of trust. If they do not know us, why should we care if they know that truth? There is no reason for them to care either way. We are trying to project a false image. Lying only separates us from the trust, truth, and intimacy that we seek. This Lawyer Mother helps us to reestablish righteousness through truth telling, opening the way to our truth. Life is about truth and consequences. With honesty within ourselves and with others we can keep all our skeletons out of the closet and speak up about all the elephants in the room!

Lawyer Mother is our spokesperson. She is a mouthpiece that speaks for us when we cannot speak up for ourselves. She teaches us how to stand up, speak up, and find our voice. She also acts in the best interest of the community, speaking up for those who do not know they even need assistance. Those who are disempowered and disenfranchised in our society need Lawyer Mother, and she is their advocate without their asking or possibly even knowing. She does it because it is the right thing to do. She does it because of her moral sense and courage.

Nkechi Taifa

Nkechi Taifa

Lawyer Mother Nkechi Taifa is a social justice attorney, advocate, activist, author, motivational speaker, and entrepreneur. I came to know her as part of our women's circle over twenty-five years ago. We developed a deeper bond by going through our pregnancies together. We were older mothers in our late thirties. At one point she had been told she could never have a child. Traditional African rituals, however, prevailed over Western medicine, and the newlyweds conceived, reaffirming that man is truly not in charge! With new babies on the way, we were waddling around together. I was due early April. She was due in early May. Even our children flipped the script on us. Her daughter was born nine days before mine, who came two weeks late. It seemed the babies already knew each other that morning when they arrived at my daughter's eighth-day naming ceremony. They have been bonded ever since, and that has bonded our family ties.

It is miraculous that Nkechi herself was even born, as her father was not supposed to survive a childhood illness and instead excelled progressing to the Olympics trials for boxing. She was the middle daughter of three children. Her parents were educated Howard University students during the Jim Crow era. Her father became a martial arts expert and instructor.

Her mission in life is to obtain justice in society. It started from reading one of her parents' books on the Emmett Till murder. This had a huge impact on her at nine years old, the lynching having occurred the year of her birth. At her young age, Nkechi had thought this type of occurrence was distant history.

In her eighth-grade black studies class, Nkechi saw Huey Newton depicted on a classroom poster and was told he was represented by white lawyers. She decided at that moment that she wanted to be a lawyer. Her inroads into law and politics occurred with her being involved in the Black Power struggle during her teenage and college years of the '60s and '70s. She felt empowered by this social action. After teaching at an African-centered private school for three years, Nkechi wanted to have the credentials to assure her standing in the larger community. Credibility being the challenge in advocating and promoting justice, she pressed forward to acquire a degree in law.

Nkechi entered the full-time evening program at George Washington University National Law Center, while working full time during the day. Her day job was advocacy against apartheid in South Africa. She worked at the Washington Office on Africa, a church-based organization located across from the US Supreme Court building, whose director was a phenomenal black woman, Jean Sindab, but she was not a lawyer. Nkechi served as office manager and network organizer for the lobbying organization. During those days, black female attorneys as role models in this area of law and advocacy were scarce. As a result, she had no mentors to counsel her in her chosen legal career.

Nkechi, an idealist new lawyer, spent the next several years as an attorney in private practice representing marginalized poor people. She witnessed youth she had successfully kept out of jail revolving in and out of the courts. She could see that her efforts were too late in the process to change the direction of this societal dilemma. It was then that Nkechi realized she wanted to work on policy to reform laws involving criminal justice. She is passionate about making things change. She has to speak out!

Nkechi, like a lot of working mothers, also struggled with work-life balance. After her marriage and the birth of her only child, she was working at the ACLU as an advocate in criminal justice. Her work required many long hours and much domestic travel. She loved her work, but she also wanted to influence the next generation of lawyers in her area of passion in law. She wanted to be the mentor for lawyers of the future, which she never had. She decided to add a focus on academia to her career. She began this focus as founding director of Howard University School of Law's award-winning Equal Justice Program. Though she later left academia, Nkechi's legacy through this program continues to give students the opportunity to engage in practical experience through volunteer legal and community service experiences. Now in the nonprofit sector, Nkechi continues her work in advocacy. She has written and spoken extensively on issues of civil/human rights and criminal and civil justice reform.

In addition to having our children together, we also went through divorce during the same time. She suggested three lawyers to me. They were like the three bears in the Goldilocks nursery rhyme. One woman thought just like me, rigid and tough, and we could be friends, but I did not think she would make a good advisor. I needed a different perspective from my own. The next attorney I interviewed seemed too soft, like a pushover. She was not up for a fight but wanted to get it over with and seemed traumatized by her own divorce. My husband was coming to play a hard ball because he did not want the divorce. The third, a gentleman, seemed just right. He seemed to have the inside track on my husband's way of thinking and could use it to my advantage. We prepared, and after serving the divorce papers, we waited the year required. He was helpful to both of us in negotiating the property and custody settlement the judge required the day of our hearing. It took less than two hours. We were divorced that day. It was a bittersweet ending and a new beginning.

Nkechi and I both were blessed and found love again quickly. The work done on forgiveness opened the door to healing to allow positive attraction. We both remarried to committed men, who keep family first. She now serves as the advocacy director for the Open Society Foundations, in the specialty area of criminal justice system reform.

The words of Fredrick Douglass keep Nkechi inspired and motivated:

> If there is no struggle, there is no progress. Those who profess to favor freedom, and yet depreciate agitation, are men who want crops without plowing up the ground. They want rain without thunder and lightning. They want the ocean without the awful roar of its many waters. This struggle may be a moral one; or it may be a physical one; or it may be both moral and physical; but it must be a struggle. Power concedes nothing without a demand. It never did and it never will.

When injustice reared its ugly head seeking my son as its next victim, Nkechi was there for me again. He was young but legally an adult. He had been minding his own business one lunchtime with some friends at a diner after completing a recording session. He was planning to go from there to work. It should have been an uneventful day. He heard some yelling from across the parking lot. He was being accused of purposefully damaging the car next to him by a white male who was being very assertive. My son did not even realize what was happening or that the man was even talking to him. Then the man began provoking him aggressively and grabbed my son. My son pushed the man away out of his face. The man announced, "You are going to jail! You have just assaulted a police officer!" Before he could blink, my son was in handcuffs. My son remained calm. The man was in plain clothes. He had never identified himself as a police officer to my son or any of his companions. It was a total shock. The whole thing was prejudiced. The white officer was only targeting a young black male to get an arrest and conviction. It would have worked, but luckily, I was able to find a good lawyer, with Nkechi's advice, who had witnesses prepared, had interviewed the accusing officer, and was ready to make a strong case.

If my son would have had to rely on a public defender without the time and resources to prepare, the story probably would have ended up quite differently—up to ten years in jail. But in this case the officer did not show up to court, and the case was dismissed. My son was exuberant with the outcome but lamented the fact that it was a financial burden to the family. It was so unfair. The reason the officer did not show up is because we did have a lawyer who could expose his lies. So many of our black males, minorities, and poor sons and daughters are being unfairly incarcerated, and frequently their white counterparts are given a pass, probation, or a slap on the wrist. My son's lawyer went back to make sure that everything regarding the arrest was expunged from his record. Many others never get a clean slate. That is why the work Nkechi is doing is so important. Even my son could have ended up a statistic.

For justice to prevail, there is the truth that needs to be spoken. There is the truth of man's law that has been agreed upon to bring forth civilizations with the stability to allow self-expression and progress without stifling creativity, which is equitable, fair, and just. This is not universal or agreed upon on planet earth and varies widely, especially in its application. Man's law has not stood the test of time. It is subject to the notions of different governments and religions. It is Lawyer Mother's belief that when man's law is in alignment with both the physical and spiritual laws of the universe, there will be consistency; there will be justice.

There are natural laws that are the physical laws of the universe in force on Mother Earth. These natural laws are living proof of our material existence, and we deal with the consequences directly. Then there are spiritual laws that affect us directly but we may be unconscious of them. If we become aware we may be able to pick up the congruencies and serendipity that allow us to realize that circumstances are not related to chance. We do create our own reality in co-creation with our fellow human brothers and sisters, and it is our responsibility to move the collective consciousness of our race forward.

Call Forth Our Higher Self

This brings to mind an old Jamaican saying, "Don't put your mouth on yourself" as a warning to watch what we are creating with our own words. The thoughts within our mind are the words we are speaking to ourselves. What are we telling ourselves? Is the recurring record playing in our mind reinforcing our self-worth, beauty, and dignity? Or do the thoughts we think and the words we speak about ourselves diminish us? Declarations that we choose to make and repeat in our minds to undo the negative voices are powerful tools that we can utilize to change our mind-set. Changing our minds can open the heart-soul connection. It leads us to a knowing with an open heart, opening the door to a righteous life.

Chapter 7

MENTOR MOTHER

OUR MENTOR MOTHER TEACHES US that it is up to us to determine our life's mission and weave that into the fabric of our life choices. She understands the energy of money and can give us the financial advice that positions us often further ahead than she has been able to go by helping us to avoid her pitfalls. She knows key people to help us and can influence those relationship connections. She also knows the nature of the people we will come into contact with and how to handle these situations. This is guidance from an expert in the field acting as our guiding light.

This wise, experienced mother is the source of good judgment and directions we can place our faith in. She has blazed the trail before us. Her experience has strengthened her with an unwavering faith. Where there is a will, there is a way, and she has found it and is willing to share with us. Her example inspires our action. When we get off course, she helps put us back on track toward our mission. She teaches us the things we did not learn in school but need to know. She knows because she has made it happen. She helps us with self-esteem, fear of failure, fear of success, and unfounded optimism.

The old African proverb "each one, teach one" speaks to the passing of the torch to the next generation.

She keeps us honest when we are lying to ourselves and others. She shows us our self-sabotage and the fear of shame that leads to our betrayal of others. She validates us, not allowing us to withdraw. She affirms us when we are faced with disappointments and frustration about the incongruences, dishonesty, and contradictions in the world. She is solution oriented, using her experience to give advice when requested. Mentor Mother is a visionary illuminated by her past experiences. We need her to keep us on track. She is our navigator, but we are at the helm. What could be better than that?

Madame Marie Currie

Madame Marie Currie

Madame Marie Currie's Journey

> All my life through, the new sights of Nature made me rejoice like a child.
>
> —Marie Curie

She became the first woman to win a Nobel Prize in science and the only person to win two Nobel prizes in two separate scientific fields, but she is inspirational because of the character she exhibited in the pursuit of her goals. She was defiant of injustice. Women were not permitted to study at the University of Warsaw in Poland. She and her older sister had to secretly meet at night in a "floating university," changing locations to avoid detection by the police. She was generous. She worked as a governess to help pay for her older sister's medical studies in Paris. In the spirit of reciprocity, her sister agreed to help cover Marie's university costs after her sister finished her studies. She was selfless, risking imprisonment by spending her spare time teaching children of Polish peasants how to read. Hungry for knowledge, she read widely, enjoying physics, math, and chemistry. She studied laboratory science, although that was forbidden by Russian authorities. She was thrifty and tenacious, saving enough money, with her sister's help, to study in Paris.

> Nothing in life is to be feared, it is only to be understood. Now is the time to understand more, so that we may fear less.
>
> —Marie Curie

Although disadvantaged by her subversive preparation, she excelled in school, completing her master's degree in physics and math in only three years. Her life supported her in expected and unexpected ways. She was awarded a scholarship in physics. She was a trailblazer. As the first woman in the world to obtain doctoral degree in science, she obtained from her research on uranium and radioactivity. She did so despite poor laboratory facilities, financial stress, and the life choices of teaching, work, marriage, and motherhood.

> One never notices what has been done; one can only see what remains to be done.
>
> —Marie Curie

Passionate and driven in the process, she and her husband, who was her scientific partner, discovered two radioactive elements she named polonium and radium. They did what had to be done to keep their home and laboratory work going. It was not until they received the Nobel Prize in physics that funding improved. She suffered rejection despite this great accomplishment when the French Academy of Science rejected her membership request in 1911.

> Be less curious about people and more curious about ideas.
>
> —Marie Curie

After her husband died in a tragic accident, she became the first woman professor at her husband's institution, where she was the first woman hired as a laboratory chief. She had to survive public scandal when she fell in love with one of her husband's students, a married man, and had an affair. His wife exposed their love letters in the press even though she and her husband had been estranged at that time. The press was deceitful, exposing her as a foreign Jewish homewrecker. She was foreign, a proud Polish woman. However, she was not Jewish, and her lover had been separated from his wife prior to their involvement.

> After all, science is essentially international, and it is only through lack of the historical sense that national qualities have been attributed to it.
>
> —Marie Curie

At this time she won her second Nobel Prize, this time in chemistry, and after that devoted her life to the Radium Institute. She was helpful during the World War effort, providing use of radiation on the front lines. With the help of donations, she assembled the fleet of twenty mobile x-ray stations as well as two hundred stationary stations. Her work later provided cutting-edge medical innovations for cancer and other ailments using radiation to destroy disease tissues.

> Life is not easy for any of us. But what of that? We must have perseverance and above all confidence in ourselves. We must believe that we are gifted for something and that this thing must be attained.
>
> —Marie Curie

Mme. Curie was admired and held in high esteem but remained humble, quiet, dignified, and unassuming. After the war she became a living legend and made the most of her fame. Her life story of her early struggles inspired more help for scientific research. She gained more support for her Radium Institute, and it became a world center for research. Later in her life she received many honorary degrees, numerous awards, and honorary memberships to societies of science throughout the world.

> I have frequently been questioned, especially by women, of how I could reconcile family life with a scientific career. Well, it has not been easy.
>
> —Marie Curie

Balancing career and family was never easy for Mme. Curie. She had the assistance of her father-in-law to help with the girls when they were young and the assistance of a Polish nanny when they were older. Her oldest daughter embraced her mother's career and went on to work with her mother at the Radium Institute. However, her youngest daughter seemed to harbor resentment for her mother until she cared for her close to her death. Mme. Curie died of aplastic anemia, which is often a result of overexposure to radiation. In the end she had sacrificed even her life for science.

> I was taught that the way of progress was neither swift nor easy.
>
> —Marie Curie

The French Academy of Sciences never inducted her into their organization. It took until 1962 for those biased men to finally induct a woman, a French physicist, Marguerite Perey, a student of Mme. Curie.

Mentor Mother is our pathfinder. She is a scout that foraged ahead to find a way others could not follow or avoided. She has looked ahead for traps and barriers and come back to help lead us. She realizes it is our own journey as we face the mountain of the challenges of our life. We confront them in the comfort of knowing somebody is willing to help us and has found a way ahead of us. She may be able to scope a better way from her perspective looking back. She may recommend an alternative route. In many cases she has walked through the fire for us so that we do not have to suffer the struggles that she faced.

Often we that follow reap the reward that she should have gained. She may have had to break "the glass ceiling" that has held all of us back. Yet there is no bitterness, just the blessing of the progress humanity has made through the manifestation of her life on planet earth. With her as our trailblazer, we can step out on faith and know we are on solid ground.

Hanna O. Sanders, MD

Hanna O. Sanders, MD

I was in a dilemma. It was my third year of medical school. I had to plan for my senior year rotation and decide on applying for residency programs. I thought I wanted to be an obstetrician gynecologist, but from my first night rotation on call I knew that I *hated* it. I was assigned to do a "pit watch" on mother of a stillborn. She was hormonally induced for labor, knowing her baby had already died. I had to go in and monitor her readings every few minutes during the hours of the ordeal. My first birth I witnessed was this stillbirth. When obstetrics is bad, it is really bad! Beyond that experience, it was too noisy, the pregnant mothers in labor were out of control, and I love to sleep too much.

So next I was sure pediatrics would be my calling. I absolutely loved the children, but their parents drove me *crazy*. I was a parent. I understood it. We lose all reason, rationality, and objectivity when our own children are sick. But I could not deal with the parents, or rather, I did not want to.

My experience of primary care was a revolving door—chasing symptoms with medications, patient noncompliance, and repeat hospitalizations. The first patient I took care of on my medicine rotation we diagnosed with colon cancer. She had ignored her symptoms for too long. We caught it too late. She returned to the medical service after her cancer surgery. She ended up passing away. Her husband and I bawled like babies. I was beginning to think I was not cut out for *any* medical career. And then I saw her, Dr. Hanna Sanders, and I said to myself, "I want to be just like her!"

I was finishing my third year and saw her on the medical ward. She was poised and confident. She commanded the attention of the attendings, residents, and staff. She was personable and friendly but a leader. She was efficient and effective and got things done. Her specialty was Physical Medicine and Rehabilitation. She prescribed exercise rather than just medication. Her patients had to take an active role in their healing process. I knew this was what I wanted. I knew this was what I was meant for. I was a health nut! I always loved exercise, nutrition, and holistic health. This was a perfect marriage of allopathic and integrative medicine—a team approach where the patient is the team leader and the Physiatrist (Physical Medicine and Rehabilitation specialist) is the coach.

Hanna's Journey

Hanna was born in San Francisco, California, before WWII. Her mother, Albertine, was a ruling force throughout her life. She worked hard and made many opportunities available for Hanna. Her stepfather adopted her shortly after WWII and was her "real" father. He arrived in her life when all of the soldiers were returning from the war. When she was five or six years old, while visiting older cousins out of town, she made her first affirmation. Her cousins would not let her play with them because she was "too young." She rebuked them by telling them, "It doesn't matter because I'm going to be a doctor when I grow up!" That was her first recollection of her desire to be a physician.

She attributes her success to loving parents, great mentors, and a good childhood education. She started with tap dance at three and piano at four. Her first piano teacher was a German immigrant. Next she was taught by Sister Miriam from the order of the Sisters of Loretta. While in high school, she also studied at the University of Southern California Preparatory School of music, and her piano teacher was Miss Dorothy Bishop. She also received strict training as a concert pianist from May Gilbert Reese and achieved her national certification at sixteen years old.

As a young black child raised in LA, she was educated in white schools most of her life. She attended Catholic education through junior high and public education in high school, and in her higher education, she was usually the only black person and frequently the only women. In California racism was covert as compared to the rest of the country, but it was still there. After graduation, while looking for her first post high school job, she was offered a job over the phone, but when she arrived, to their surprise, as a Negro, she was not hired. She was encouraged by her mother to pursue a nurse's training degree at LA County Hospital School of Nursing. She quit nurse's training after two years of a three-year program. She did not want to be a nurse! She, however, continued her education, enrolling at Los Angeles City College, with emphasis in music and biological sciences. She married and continued to work and go to school. In 1966 she had her only child.

As a working wife and mother of a young son, she attended LA City College, majoring in music and biology. She received her associate's degree and transferred to California State University at Los Angeles, where she pursued her goals in biological science and music. She was mentored by Dr. Alberscheim in the music department and Dr. Vance in the zoology department. She received a BS in zoology with a music minor. She was encouraged to go on and pursue a graduate degree. This was 1968/9 at the forefront of affirmative action for women, blacks, and other minorities, such as people of Hispanic descent. She entered graduate school at USC in an MS/PHD program in anatomy. Her mentor in graduate school was Dr. Sol Bernick, a renowned histo-anatomist, publishing over five hundred papers in the field. She worked with him for four years. She was teaching anatomy to medical and dental students at that time. She was finishing up her experiments and thesis when she got into medical school at The University of California, Irvine (UCI).

Her medical education was not academically challenging to her but was mentally and emotional challenging because she no longer had mentors. This was only the second year of accepting blacks and women in any numbers into UCI Medical School. She was one of a handful of women and blacks in her graduating class, graduating in three years.

Dr. Jerome Tobis, Physical Medicine and Rehabilitation (PM&R) founding chairman and professor in the Department of PM&R at UC Irvine, inspired her career in Physiatry. It was a natural for her because physiatrists look at the whole person not persons separated into organ systems. There is a focus on physical and mental functioning in all the roles of one's life: personal, social, and work life. Physiatrists provide integrated services, working as a team. Although physiatrists take care of all age groups of patients, her interest was gerontology and the older adults in rehabilitation. She entered his residency program, where she met Dr. David Simons and Dr. Janet Travell as a second-year resident. They introduced her to myofascial pain and the physical medicine techniques in the treatment of its problems, including trigger point injections and manual muscle manipulations.

She was fifteen years my senior when we met. She was a single parent and had just completed her board certification in physical medicine and rehabilitation. She joined the medical and academic staff at Howard University in Washington, DC, and was just beginning a private practice. She was delighted to talk to me about her field. She was knowledgeable and excited. She had worked with ground-breaking physicians in the field demonstrating cutting-edge techniques in pain management and patient care. She had faced personal and career challenges with dignity, integrity, and compassion. I had left the city to do my residency under her wise counsel and didn't wait for a, long-awaited, local program to start. It started late and ended badly, and luckily, I avoided that pitfall.

I followed in Hanna's footsteps, coming out of my residency and taking her position when she returned back out west as a staff physiatrist and associate professor with a part-time private practice. I quickly got caught up in the politics of academic medicine. I had a small research grant and was doing good work, but I was not happy. I had a dream to move the university forward. A lot was happening to change medical education at the major universities, and I felt we could lead the way. However, the university was staunch in its traditions. The times were changing, and we as an institution were not keeping up. My dream was my own integrative private musculoskeletal practice, but I wanted to make a mark and give back.

I was a good team player and could rally the troops. I was selected to lead the quality assurance committee for the department and was doing a bang-up job. However, the administration didn't like the cold hard facts, especially before our accreditation revue. In good conscience, with the advice of my mentor, I had to step down. I had planned to stay three years, but I stubbornly wore out my welcome after five years before I went into full-time private practice.

Hanna was key on making that transition. She invited me out to her practice in Palm Springs to show me the ropes. I gained insight and experience from her myofascial techniques. She pushed me into leadership roles in the NMA following in her footsteps, handing me the torch for that PM&R section leadership and my role in health care transitions for the Americans with Disabilities Act. She helped me build a CV that would lead to my current employment as Medical Director of a Physiatry Department. She has managed life's twists and turns of relationship, career, and health challenges and has done it with grace and perseverance. She is an inspiration and a role model.

We still managed to see each other at medical meetings regularly until she slowed down into semi-retirement. She has been a friend and mentor to me over the years, and now I hope to be that for others as well. I started the Physiatry Department at my institution and take a personal interest in the success of our department, the practitioners and staff, and our organization as a whole. Hanna has taught me loving leadership and personable service, the skill I use to promote its growth and foster in the next generation of physiatrists. Her mission in life: "To be an upright person and help people as much as I can. Being a doctor is only one way I can fulfill this mission." — Hanna O. Sanders, MD

My Mentor Mothers have given me the perspective to look at each person as an experiment of one. We all have opportunities to experience an experiment within our own life. We have different outcomes by taking opportunities and risks to challenge our habitual life patterns of thinking and doing. My personal and career satisfaction has come because failure has become a path to knowledge and not an obstacle. While I never expect not to make mistakes, I know life is a perfect expression of the evolution of the human spirit. We are all on a mission. We are all evolving. We all make a difference.

These Mentor Mothers' lives of purpose can be an example to help us live a life of purpose. What makes our heart sing? What do we enjoy doing so much that we would do it even if we did not get paid? How can our work feed our soul as well as fill our pocketbook? Living a life of purpose and meaning by being of service and making our mark in the history of humanity is important to nurture our passions. The goal is to live a rich and full life.

Chapter 8

Sexy Mama

How do we sustain the courage to manifest the largest possible dream for ourselves regardless of our fears? This mother shows us the ability to be reflective so we can take action toward actualization of our dreams. She is a seer. She gives us insight that allows us to see meaningful visions for our own life. These allow us to spark our imagination, develop our talent, and express our originality. We let our creative imagination run free. We begin to know ourselves and others as a part of the vast resource of the universe, where all competition, jealousy, and envy disintegrate. We become aware that creativity is spiritual energy we all have. By transforming conscious creative thoughts to powerful, passionate feeling by inner reflection, we can learn a way of being in "the flow" of the rhythm of life. But like a wave we ride, we realize that we don't stay at that peak. When the tide recedes, we again spend time preparing for the next wave to come along.

Our Sexy Mother is a lover. She shows us how to come into ourselves through the expression of the senses. Her power is seductive. Beautiful, erotic, and passionate, she does not abuse her sexual energy because it is a sacred energy at the heart of the creative power of the universe. Yet she shows us our sexual energy is another exquisite opportunity to experience our deep perception of being fully alive. She makes us hungry for life itself!

Access Universal Information

She brings out our inherent capabilities. We learn ways of visualization, meditation, connection, and surrender. She teaches us our thoughts and emotions are active and not passive and that we do not need anyone else to validate us but ourselves. With her energy, we bounce back from despair, inferiority, and opposition in the service of virtue, ingenuity, and love.

Her guidance reminds us how to make daydreaming a step toward actualization, energizing the images by indulging in joy and pleasure to arouse our life force. However, there is a warning against overindulgence that weakens and wastes our life energy. This Sexy Mama can help us turn around negative memories from regrets to learning experiences as powerful tools to propel us forward. She stirs our imagination through the use of metaphors, myths, storytelling, symbols, and proverbs, giving us a new picture to go on.

Growing up I was looking for my place in the family. My brother's the oldest and only boy. That is all he needed for his claim to fame. My oldest sister was the boss. She was in charge of my middle sister and me. My middle sister was the pretty one. I was too "light skinned" and too "skinny." I was teased for my skinny legs, and they were called "bamboo" shooting down from my wide baby-making hips out of my hot pants, which was the style when I was a teenager. I decided to be smart! I got good grades in school and always had some minor fact to blurt out on any dinner table subject. It worked. My siblings nicknamed me Super Brain. I craved adult attention as well. I studied all the dance moves on *Soul Train*. I was always called on, to my delight, to show my parents' friends the latest dances.

I always wanted to study dance, but my parents could not afford it when I was a child. I wanted to be graceful. I and my soul sister Joye were the party girls at my college. Joyful and skillful at popular dances, we were invited by special invitation to all the happening parties each weekend because we love to dance and we were never wallflowers. If the music was right, we got the party started. I took up Middle Eastern belly dance in undergraduate school, and my teacher recommended ballet. The ballet helped my belly dance posture, alignment, and presence. Later I took and taught North African belly dance and still continue to practice and refine my skills. I liked the sensuality of dance, the allure, and the creativity. Meanwhile I learned West African dance with my daughter in a community dance class and performed with her in the dance company shows as she was growing up. It has been said "drummers dance with their hands and dancers drum with their feet." I dance because the song is in my heart! This is just one reason why Josephine Baker inspires me.

Josephine Baker

JOSEPHINE BAKER

BEFORE LUCILLE BALL'S PHYSICAL COMEDY, before Madonna's sensational performances, and before Angelina Jolie's inspiring international adoption, there was Josephine Baker, funny girl, sex symbol, mother of the "Rainbow Tribe," and much, much, more. She was called Black Venus, Black Pearl, and Creole Goddess. Her career spanned fifty years. She lived her life passionately, and though her road took many ups and downs and twists and turns, she chose her course with enthusiasm.

Enthusiasm and Positive Attitude-

> Beautiful? It's all a question of luck. I was born with good legs. As for the rest … beautiful, no. Amusing, yes.
>
> —Josephine Baker

Her parents had a song and dance act. She was abandoned by her father and raised in poverty by her mother. She was abused as a live-in domestic at eight years old. She survive the race riots of St. Louis in 1917. She dropped out of school at the age of thirteen and worked waitressing. She started working comedy on Vaudeville at the age of fifteen. She came to New York City during the Harlem Renaissance. She started out as a dresser for a dance troupe after she was rejected as a dancer for being "too dark" and "too skinny." She worked behind the scenes and learned the routines, and when a dancer left, she seized that opportunity. She became her replacement. Her style was overt, over the top, and attention-getting, as she purposefully rolled her eyes and acted clumsy. Her comedy became a box office draw.

Sensuality/ Sexuality-

> I improvised, crazed by the music … Even my teeth and eyes burned with fever. Each time I leaped I seemed to touch the sky and when I regained earth it seemed to be mine alone.
>
> —Josephine Baker

She became an overnight sensation when she left New York and went to Paris, France. In her new act, she wore only a feathered skirt, and her salacious movements drove the audiences wild. She lived lavishly, with exotic pets, clothing, and jewelry. Her famous "banana dance" flagged her celebrity status. She was one of the most photographed women in the world. By the age of twenty-one, she earned more than any other entertainer in Europe and starred in two movies by her late twenties. She had married twice before she left the United States and had over fifteen hundred marriage proposals in France and many affairs.

Charm-

> I did take the blows [of life], but I took them with my chin up, in dignity, because I so profoundly love and respect humanity.
>
> —Josephine Baker

Her return to the United States in 1936 proved a disaster. White American audiences rejected and denigrated her, calling her "Negro wench." She returned to France heartbroken. She married a Frenchman and gave up her US citizenship. However, that marriage did not last. She worked for the French military intelligence during World War II. Her celebrity status allowed her to rub elbows with the elite of Europe gather information and get it to the French underground. She would smuggle secret messages in her music sheets. She also performed for the troops. She was awarded the Medal of the Resistance and Chevalier of the Legion of Honor by the French government for her heroic work for the French people in World War II.

Creativity

> I believe in prayer. It's the best way we have to draw strength from heaven.
>
> —Josephine Baker

At the age of forty-three, she reinvented herself and reestablished herself as one of Paris's foremost entertainers. At forty-five she was invited back to the United States to perform. She was active in breaking the color barrier by refusing to entertain at any club or theater not integrated. She won battles to desegregate the nightclub audiences. She performed to sold-out audiences in her national tour. The NAACP named May 20 Josephine Baker Day in honor of her civil rights efforts. Honored as NAACP's Woman of the Year with a parade in the Harlem, things looked bright until an incident in the Stork Club. She criticized the club's unwritten policy of discrimination she suffered as a black patron. Influential columnist Walter Winchell, a witness to the events, rather than rising to her defense accused her of being a communist sympathizer during the time of the McCarthy hearings. The negative publicity ended up in her being forced out of the United States to return to France.

Femininity/Fertility

> Surely the day will come when color means nothing more than the skin tone, when religion is seen uniquely as a way to speak one's soul; when birth places have the weight of a throw of the dice and all men are born free, when understanding breeds love and brotherhood.
>
> —Josephine Baker

After World War II, she married a French composer. Unable to have children of her own, Josephine Baker adopted twelve children from around the world of difference ethnicities and religions. With this Rainbow Tribe, she wanted to prove to the world that we all could be brothers and sisters in one human family. She vowed to make her home a model of world brotherhood. This parenting effort combined with the expenses of her castle in France led to divorce, bankruptcy, and her being physically removed from their home at the age of fifty-eight. The princess of Monaco, former actress Grace Kelly, offered her a home near Monaco to raise her children.

Grace/Beauty

> The secret to the fountain of youth is to think youthful thoughts.
>
> —Josephine Baker

At sixty-two, she revived her career in Europe. Five years later she returned triumphantly to the United States, performing at Carnegie Hall and receiving a standing ovation before her performance. Humbled, she wept. In Paris she opened a show celebrating her fifty years in show business to glowing reviews.

Dramatic Exit

> I love performing. I shall perform until the day I die.
>
> —Josephine Baker

Four days later she was found peacefully in a coma after suffering a stroke surrounded by newspaper articles of her performance. Over twenty thousand people packed the streets of Paris to watch her funeral procession. She received full French military honors at her funeral, making her the first American-born woman to receive that honor.

Dorothy Bernal

Dorothy Bernal

Dorothy Bernal is my Sexy Mama. My mama has always been a "hot" mama. She had always known how to make the most of her assets. She was a small woman, thin and short with tiny feet. She was no "Brick House" but made the most of what she had and taught, encouraged, and gifted her daughters to do the same. She has shared all of Victoria's secrets, and I have the drawers full of garments and lingerie to prove it.

She and the women of her generation were too shy to talk to us directly about sex and did so with subtle innuendo and meaningful mentioning. We got her points. We learned about our budding womanhood from a book I'll never forget called *Growing up and Liking It*. It had been handed down through my two older sisters before me. All I could remember was I was *not* liking it.

I was the consummate tomboy. I liked to play boy games in the neighborhood with the boys and my tomboy girlfriend, Kathy. But at fourteen my body stopped cooperating with me. I was as skinny as a rail, flat as a pancake, but all of a sudden, it seemed like out of nowhere my hips jutted out the sides of my body like saucers. When the big bowl game of neighborhood football came, I left revved up and came home victorious, on an exuberant high. I got home just in time to clean up for supper. My mommy, my two sisters, and I shared the girls' bathroom freely. When my mom came in and saw the black and blue bruises covering my saucers, she swiftly declared, "Your football-playing days are over!" I was in shock! My bubble burst. My life would be changed forever. It was so much so fast. It all slipped away.

We never formally addressed my changing to young womanhood,

but she showed me by example how to embrace my changing form. When money could not afford the latest fashion trends, she bought me patterns and material for me to use the sewing talents I learned in 4H club to show off my newfound figure. She encouraged a sensual sophistication. While I never inherited her love of shopping or shoe fetish, I still do like to show my own unique style in the clothes I wear. We share a love for bright colors, especially red hot red. Now I inherited her skinny legs and her beautiful looks. Of all my siblings, I look the most like my mother. I love dresses and skirts more than pants or shorts and a man to open the door, stand when I enter a room, and tip his hat. My mother, Carol, and I love hats. They just complete a look, and I do have the hat boxes to prove that. It took a minute, but I now do enjoy being a lady!

My mother, like the generations before her, has always felt a person's body should be light upon his or her soul. She has always enjoyed a slim figure and the pleasure of good food right at the perfect temperature, but never to excess. When I returned from a summer abroad as an AFS foreign exchange student to Australia, she was determined to get those newly found twenty-two pounds of fish and chips off of me. She drove me to the Elaine Powers women's fitness studio to exercise every evening Monday through Friday after my dinner salad. And that salad was all I had for dinner for the six weeks it took me to lose that weight. While I never did pick up the art of makeup, shopping, or high heels, I did pick up the art of sensuality from my birth mother. At eighty she was still red hot, sassy, and sexy!

My mother Immigrated to the United States from Jamaica with two babes in arms, fifteen-month-old girl Yvonne and thirty-month-old boy Patrick. She was leaving everyone she ever knew and all of her family with the goal of making a better life for her children. When she arrived, her sister-in-law, Aunt Pearlie, gave her crystal glasses that she always kept in the china cabinet. It was a gift to remember her by, meeting her new family in a new land. She loved formal glasses, china, and beautiful things. She dreamed of a china cabinet full but got these things many years later after she got her children settled. She had two more children after she arrived, my sister Carol and myself, the baby of the family. Life was a financial struggle, and my mother wanted to provide beautiful things for her little boy and three girls. She washed clothes daily to make sure her children were clean and well dressed. She wanted more! Quite to my father's chagrin, she decided to go to work outside the home.

She applied at the Industrial Rayon Factory for work. Many of the other Jamaican women immigrants also worked there. It was hard assembly line work, requiring heavy lifting on an assembly line. She was initially refused the job, because of her petite size, but convinced them to give her a week trial to see if she could handle it. "You try me. You'll see!" she requested. The first day she was singing a different tune. After standing all day and pulling heavy bolts of cords, her back hurt, her arms were sore, and her feet ached. A female worker she met in the locker room that first day recommended supportive shoes and a support girdle for the job, and she never looked back. She grew stronger the longer she worked in the job. Despite full-time work, she remained the full-time homemaker as well.

She started on the night shift. They could not afford a babysitter. My siblings and I were not all in school full days. I not-so-fondly remember my mother braiding our hair so tight at night we had slanted eyes. She wrapped our heads with scarves so we were presentable in the mornings. Every evening she laid out the ironed clothes we were to put on in the morning. Then my father would prepare our breakfast and get us off to school before he left for work as my mother arrived home from work. When my sister Carol and I arrived home after our shorter day, she would be there to take care of us. She would put us down for our nap while she slept. Her naps lasted longer than ours. We would occasionally get in trouble from making a mess doing projects from *Romper Room* or *Captain Kangaroo*. She worked rotating shiftwork for a while. Rotating every two weeks from day shift to swing shift (afternoons) and then night shift was discombobulating. The idea of this schedule was to distribute the stress of the less-desirable swing and night shifts across the entire work force. Whoever thought of that schedule for factory workers didn't know anything about one's biological clock. That was the worst! When production went down across the board, her factory luckily changed back to the three fixed shifts again. When we were all in school full days and she had put in enough time to have the seniority, she was able to bid for and get a job on day shift. We still got our hair braided at night, and she organized our clothing because she had to leave early for the day shift before we awakened. And through every shift change, she always had dinner on the table for us to sit down as a family by 6:00 p.m. sharp. Her boss never had to say a word to her about her performance until she retired, job well done, after twenty-one years when the factory closed and moved offshore in 1980.

Like a good Jamaican, that was not her only job. She sold Avon from the time she started working until the age of eighty-five. She was a volunteer assistant at the senior center for twenty years and taught crochet classes. She also served for many years as a minister of hospitality at her church. She was a role model for hard and productive work and a life of meaningful service.

> Don't have any more children than you can afford to raise yourself.
>
> —Dorothy Bernal

My father was old school and never wanted his wife to work. He was not a grateful husband. It was the time of women's liberation and the cold war between the United States and USSR. And that cold war played out in my parents' relationship as my mother gained more financial freedom. But she could always melt his cold heart with her sassy, sexy, sensual ways. They had a shared mission to get us into Catholic school for a good education and afford the clothing we needed. My mother liked to dress her children cute! She controlled her own income and worked together with Dad to negotiate who paid what bills. Her income afforded special occasion hairdos by a hairdresser, groceries, rare family vacations, and finally after years of saving, a second car—her blue Pontiac LeMans. There were times when she was tempted to return to Jamaica and tempted to leave her marriage. But there was no need. When the safety and security of the children came into question, my parents always managed to get back on the same page. It took boldness to stand up for herself and her family to seek employment.

Don't be a Poop Stick!

—Dorothy Bernal

My parents came to Painesville, Ohio, from Jamaica with waves of my Uncle Karl and Aunt Pearlie's friends and relatives. The small black community was not very welcoming of them, and the white community in the '50s weren't very sociable either. The small Jamaican network of family friends were mostly factory workers, and on the weekends, it was party time. They planned during the week who would host that weekend's parties. There were a lot of parties among the Painesville Jamaicans locally or there were adventures to parties at friends' homes in Cleveland thirty miles away. On special occasions, there were formal affairs. I would love to see my mom prepare our home for parties or dress up for these social events. My mother was a party animal. She loved to go out and dress up, a social butterfly. My dad was the opposite, quiet, private, and reserved. Opposites attract! She had a funny way of making her own sayings from US slang. A "stick in the mud" and a "party pooper" became a "poop stick!" She would frequently have to coax my dad when he was being a poop stick!

Straighten up!

—Dorothy Bernal

My mother had a serious postural pet peeve. My mother would take her index finger knuckle and press it on our spine between our shoulder blades if we were slouching to make us sit up straight. We sat at the kitchen table for meals, homework, and socializing. She would pass by and give us a poke so often that when we heard her coming, we automatically stuck those girls up and out. Later we just got stuck that way. My mom had beautiful posture and her own runway stroll she used as she sashayed through the grocery store aisles, the factory floor, or the entrance to the ball, with her head held high, her shoulders back, and her arms straight and flung open wide. She moved forward from her hips, gliding side to side. One day I mentioned to a friend, as we walked behind my daughter and mother who was visiting at the shopping mall, "Wow, Afryea walks just like her grandmother." She said to me, "Afryea walks just like *her* mother!" Who knew! I thought it had skipped a generation!

When busy with household tasks, my mother moved swiftly. After all, on Thursdays when the good food arrived at the market before the week's coupons expired, she had three stores to hit and still get dinner on the table by six. She was brilliant but never recognized or acknowledged what cognitive skill it took to organize three stores' coupons and keep the week's prices in her head to get things at the cheapest price from each of the stores, while planning all the three meals for the seven days for a family of six in that one whirlwind shopping trip. I never appreciated her talents until I was much older trying to keep my own small family organized.

But she slowed down when going out on the town. She glided gracefully and leisurely allowed herself to be seen from head to toe. She knew how to but an outfit together, matching the exact style, color and shade. She has grown more beautiful over time. The picture I included here is a drawing I did of my mother through the ages in honor of my mommy's eighty-fifth birthday. It is from pictures of her around twenty, fifty, and eighty years old. Over the years, I learned to value my mother's wisdom, sensuality, and beauty that had embarrassed me growing up. After all she was "old" to me back then. I dedicated this simple poem to her at her eighty-fifth birthday party:

Mommy

Your beauty—ageless.
Your devotion—fearless.
Your wisdom—timeless.
Your rice and peas—flawless.
Your spirit—limitless.
Your shopping—endless.
The depths of my love for you—bottomless.
Your love for us—priceless.

Sexy Mama helps us because she is a dreamer. She thrives on her inner vision, and she manifests her dreams. She helps us see our vision in life and gives us the boldness to go for it! She helps us step out in confidence even if we have to fake it to make it at first. Otherwise we may escape into hiding. We can be so inspired by our purpose but have a fear of being "out there," vulnerable. We can get so overwhelmed and intimidated by our vision that we want to disappear. Hopelessness can keep us frozen. We can lose our sense of purpose, leaving us lost in the wilderness. This Sexy Mama helps us keep our dream alive. She holds our dreams for us when we are too tired, scared, or defeated to dream. She shows us how to awaken all of our senses to enliven the dream in every cell of our being. She shakes us up and wakes us up. She stirs our enthusiasm, helping us to stand up for ourselves and have a positive attitude.

> When you are satisfied, you are dead.
>
> —Dorothy Bernal

We build on the legacy of our ancestors. My maternal grandfather was a government worker in Kingston, Jamaica. He also loved to dress professionally with suits and ties and shoes polished. My mother was the last of seven children born to my grandparents. Her four older brothers survived, and two girl children had passed as infants. She was their long-awaited baby girl. They felt the city life was too hazardous for their precious girl child and sent her to live with her aunties in the country. She had a tantrum at six years old and refused to go back with her aunts after a visit. Her older brothers were working and spoiled her with suede sandals when her father gave her big, ugly boots from the shoemaker because he felt she was hard on shoes. She loved beautiful shoes ever since, and with tiny size five feet, she had a closet full. To call my mother a clothes horse is not an exaggeration but a description. But she was a bargain shopper and got every bang for her buck. Her mother was estranged from most of her Jewish family, who disowned her for marring a Catholic black man. She converted from Judaism to Catholicism to be married in my granddad's church. My maternal grandmother had to vow to raise her children Catholic, and my father did also when he married my mom.

My father was a friend of my mother's older brother. Six years her senior, he must have swept her off her feet. They were together a tumultuous fifty-one years until my father's passing. It was the only life she knew as an adult, but she was able to live on her own for her next fifteen years. She had never lived on her own before. She went from her parents' house to her marital home. Then she lived in the mother-in-law suite in my sister's Yvonne's home.

We have not had the challenges of our grandfather. Neither have we had the struggles of our parents, who immigrated to the United States from Jamaica during the era of Jim Crow and segregation. These middle-class factory workers were able to achieve their goal of having their four children graduate from college. We all were always told that we could be anything we wanted to be and do what we wanted to do, despite the social context of the racism of the time. Fortunately, the civil rights movement was part of the groundswell that carried us.

My Sexy Mama had passion and did what needed to be done to manifest her dreams and for us to manifest ours. She kept the vision of our goal for her children's future. So when my brother dropped out of college, she influenced his return to school when his second sister four years his junior was about to graduate from college before him. After graduation when he wanted to go back and work in the factory, she forced him to go out and look for a "real" job. She encouraged me, during all my ups and downs of medical training, to never give up the vision and keep my eyes on the prize. She and my father helped my brother to raise his teenage son in our family home, when my nephew's mother let him come live with his dad.

She helped Carol return to work after her second child was born when she could not find somebody she trusted to take care of her two children when it was time for her to return to work. She moved to Chicago to care for them until they were twelve and fifteen years old. She and my dad moved to Atlanta to be in a warmer climate closer to my oldest sister, Yvonne. She was steadfastly holding the vision of her oldest daughter Yvonne's teaching career to get her master's and doctorate and follow her dreams of becoming a school principal.

> It takes all kinds to make world.
>
> —Dorothy Bernal

I called my mother every Sunday afternoon through my extensive education so we would always be in touch and she never had to worry. Then we naturally continued these conversations through my entire adult life until her illness prevented it. There were times when I complained about parenting and children. As I was her smart aleck child, her only reply was, "God has a sense of humor!" There were times when I called her, discouraged or perplexed. The advice I always heard was, "It takes all kinds to make world." No matter what the circumstance, I wanted reality or people to be different. She wanted me to realize that it was what it was, no matter what I thought it should be. This was very grounding to me—a reality check that the only kind of person I could choose was the one kind of person I chose to be. What kind of person was I? How was I choosing to make my world?

Living My Dream

I apologized to my mommy when I was in my sophomore year of college, again after the birth of my first child, and again when my kids were teenagers. I have worked for over twenty-five years with adolescents in rite-of-passage programs and over five years in my sorority's high school youth mentoring programs. Maybe it is my way of being part of the village for these teenagers and help take some of the burden from their parents. No one can be all things to anyone. In living my life's purpose, I wish to find meaning by being of service. The counsel of my Sexy Mama helps me do just that. She has the fuel that feeds the flame for our life's passions!

> Good friends are better than pocket money!
>
> —my mother's favorite Jamaican proverb

My mother departed this life at the age of eighty-eight. She had a beautiful home going at her Catholic Church. She had the funeral mass she wanted that was attended by family and her many good friends. In my spiritual tradition, taught to me by my spiritual Queen Mother, I held a forty-day ancestral ritual that was key to my healing process. The preparation for this allowed me to transition from the grief of her death to the celebration of her life. It occurred forty days after her death. I prepared a beautiful program filled with pictures and happy memories and the story of her life well lived. My daughter prepared a beautiful slide show with pictures from my mother's life from her childhood, through her lifetime, to our most recent memories. I prepared all of her favorite foods with her favorite recipes: Ackee and saltfish, roast breadfruit, and fried plantain with sliced tomato and avocado, escovitch fish with rice and peas, callaloo, and stir fry cabbage. I served her favorite drinks: Bombay Sapphire gin and tonic, Heineken beer, sorrel, and ginger beer. For dessert there was Jamaican bread pudding with rum sauce and coconut grater cake.

I invited my friends to share in the evening with me so I could honor her memory and share her legacy. I prepared the tables with beautiful place settings and décor. We listened to her favorite music—calypso, soca, reggae, and definitely Harry Belafonte! We prayed. I served the food hot, right at 6:00 p.m., like she had served me from her table all of my life. We were breaking bread with my mother, and it was a Jamaican feast. After reflection on her life and personal reflections from friends and family members, I shared the portrait I did for her and her poem. We hung my mother's picture next to my father's picture on our ancestral wall. We ended with a musical tribute "The Best of Tom Jones," her favorite musical artist. He was the sex symbol of her day, and she was my Sexy Mama! I completed her final rite of passage into the spiritual world as a revered and respected ancestor.

Chapter 9

WARRIOR MOTHER

WARRIOR MOTHERS MANIFEST COURAGE. SHE put our well-being before her own well-being, risking even life itself for her children. She does not do this haphazardly. She is strategic and avoids danger with good preplanning. But if the situation arises, she is at the ready. She is energetic, prudent, forceful, enterprising, constructive, skillful, passionate, and motivated. She swiftly responds, not reacts, to challenging situations, which are hard and dangerous but usually resolve rapidly and hopefully do not occur frequently. The difference between responding and reacting is crucial. When we react, the situation is in control of us. When we respond, we are in control of the situation. In this way, our Warrior Mother makes sure her zealousness and courage is being directed by her higher moral spiritual self.

The warrior energy is to right wrongs. It is the balancing of energy. Warrior Mother Energy can be helpful for guarding against an enemy or against us becoming an antagonist in a situation we have the power to defuse. Within ourselves we have the power to control our arrogant attitudes, our impetuous impulses, our destructive behaviors, our forceful personalities, our excessive compulsions, our worrying and complaining, overzealous urges, and rash actions that can lead to violence. When we need help, Warrior Mother will assure us there is a cavalry on the way! I have to call in my team for backup. When I need help out of the holes I have dug for myself, I call on the healers to help me heal.

I recently lost my psychiatrist of over twenty years. We have known each other professionally for a decade before that, and I have known of her work even a decade earlier still. I did not need to see her often after we established the intimacy of our doctor-patient relationship. But if I felt myself sinking, she would send me a lifeline that could help lift me out of my stinking thinking. Another healer is my psychologist. My psychologist does cognitive behavioral therapy. We do not just talk about my problems; we develop strategies for resolution. I have received spiritual guidance from my priests over the years. From them I obtain the direction, compassion, nurturing, hope, and love I need to move forward. This sacred space gives me a safe place to vent and transform negativity.

Every week during my divorce, I went to my priests for divorce counseling. It was like letting the steam out of the pressure cooker that had built up over the week. I was able to release ungodly thoughts and come to a place of self-forgiveness that allowed me to give forgiveness to others. I know there can be a stigma in people's minds about needing mental health services, but I want to feel good. I know I feel much better when I get the help I need, whether it is from self-help books, healing retreats, or counseling, or when seeking guidance from one of my mothers in my Mothers' Council. This is my cavalry, and it is a big and diverse group of comrades. I always feel better when my backup crew gets me back into my right mind.

Warrior Mother understands the battle with the enemy within and the enemies outside of us. She knows that if you do not exorcise the demons within, the demons outside will not be able to haunt us. Warrior Mother is a righteous warrior. She focuses on protecting her inner circle—herself, her children, and her family—and once secured, her efforts are broadened to the larger community and society. For communal threats, she encourages the collective work and responsibility of the entire group. She realizes that she must be ready at a moment's notice and laziness will keep her off guard. She is preparing us to be warriors ourselves. Warrior Mother is inspiring. She demonstrates perseverance, standing up for herself and others. She is honorable and willing to take a stand.

Joan of Arc

Joan of Arc

Joan's Journey

> I was in my thirteenth year when I heard a voice from God to help me govern my conduct. And the first time I was very much afraid.
>
> —Joan of Arc

She walked in her father's garden for years, but imagine her surprise at the age of thirteen when Joan heard voices. She was afraid and probably confused and concerned, asking herself where the voices were coming from. She was told that the messages were from God through Saint Michael the Archangel, St. Catherine, and St. Margaret, and she most likely kept this information close to her heart at first. Imagine her surprise when she then received a vision of the Archangel Michael. When she was told she must lead Charles VII to his coronation at Reims, was she alarmed? Did she know? Had she heard of the prophecy that foretold that France would be saved by a maid from Lorraine? This prediction was well known in France during Joan's time and had been attributed to several prophets. But as a young girl, had Joan heard of this prophecy?

Born to a peasant family in the north of France, Jeanette was the youngest daughter of a farmer and a devoutly Catholic mother, with three older brothers and a much older sister. She refused to be married and spoke a vow of celibacy. Emboldened by her voices and visions, she left home at sixteen to answer her calling. She first traveled to Vaucouleuers to see Sir Robert de Baudricourt. It took three trips to him before he agreed to assist her. What convinced him to risk his reputation by supporting this persistent young woman?

Act, and God will act.

—Joan of Arc

She traveled eleven days and 375 miles through enemy territory, disguised as a man with her hair cut short and wearing men's clothing, in the late winter of 1429 to see Charles VII. There was no way she could have had knowledge of his looks, so Charles tested her by hiding himself among a crowd at his court, but Joan immediately found him. She was able to recognize him with the help of her voices. Skeptical still, he had Joan physically examined by ladies of the court to prove she was a virgin. Then she was questioned by church officials for three weeks. After the examination, finally convinced, he officially gave her command of the army of France. Joan of Arc is the youngest known person in history to command the army of any nation. She was only seventeen, a young woman with no military training.

I am not afraid … I was born to do this.

—Joan of Arc

She led her army to Orleans in late April 1429 to lift the English siege. She led with authority. She had purged her army camps of prostitutes, treachery, and gambling, driving these distractors away at sword point. She disciplined prominent knights for indecent behavior, foul language, or missing Mass. She called out those countrymen, accusing them of being "spineless," and admonished them when they tried to dismiss her battle plans. Her strategy was brilliant and faultless. Joan carried a banner with the picture of God and the words *Jesus* and *Mary* written on it leading the men into battle. She wore a suit of armor but carried no weapon. A siege lasting years had ended by her military tactics, leadership directing troops, and inspiration in only three days of fighting. She progressed promptly from battlefield to battlefield, overwhelming a better armed and outnumbered enemy. Though she proposed diplomatic solutions, these were rejected by the English. Joan predicted she would be wounded by an arrow to the shoulder above her breast in a letter dated fifteen days before the event. This was in the exact manner that it occurred. The people of Orleans began calling Joan the Maid of Orleans after that famous battle of Orleans.

> Since God had commanded it, it was necessary that I do it. Since God commanded it, even if I had a hundred fathers and mothers, even if I had been a King's daughter, I would have gone nevertheless.
>
> —Joan of Arc

Her greatest military victory was at Patay on June 18, 1429. Her army annihilated the English forces, killing over two thousand while suffering almost no losses. She had to cross enemy territory and take the town by force to enable the king's coronation. Joan Crowned Charles VII king of France on July 17, 1429, in the great cathedral of Reims. Joan fulfilled the central part of her mission when Charles VII was crown king. Joan was rewarded by Charles with a coat of arms. The victory was considered a miracle. Her reputation spread far and wide.

She attempted to liberate Paris on September 8, 1429. The attempt failed, and she was wounded after a long day of fighting. She was hit by a bolt from a crossbow on her thigh. She refused to leave the battle until she was forcibly carried to the rear. Joan wanted to move forward immediately since their army had the momentum and she wanted to press forward to retake Paris. The new king wavered. He was warned by others in his court that Joan was becoming too powerful. She wanted to renew the attack the next day but was overruled by Charles. She spent the winter of 1429 as a frustrated guest in the king's court. She waited impatiently, giving their enemies in Paris time to fortify their position.

> One life is all we have and we live it as we believe in living it. But to sacrifice what you are and to live without belief, that is a fate more terrible than dying.
>
> —Joan of Arc

She was captured in spring of 1430, when the king ordered her to attack the city of Compiegne. Joan had taken the field with a small army. She had been thrown off her horse outside the gates of the city as the drawbridge closed. Despite a fight, she was captured by Burgundian soldiers May 23, 1430. She was taken to a castle occupied by the English. She escaped by leaping from a tower and survived the sixty-foot fall but was knocked unconscious and recaptured. She was betrayed by her traitorous countrymen and sold to England for ten thousand gold francs.

She was in captivity for a year. Abandoned, the French army did not come to rescue her, nor did her King Charles try to negotiate her release. The English paid for a trial run by corrupt church officials loyal to them. Taken to Rouen in the spring of 1431, she was put on trial for heresy. Held in a prison cell, Joan was shackled to her bed. By the convention of the day, she should have been held in a church, guarded by women. But the English kept her closely guarded by their soldiers and refused to allow her to be held at the church.

> You say that you are my judge; I do not know if you are; but take good heed not to judge me ill, because you would put yourself in great peril.
>
> —Joan of Arc

The English court attempted penetrating questioning during the trial, but Joan remained silent throughout the examination. Enraged, her jailors threatened her with torture unless she renounced her actions and disavowed her voices and visions. Accused of over seventy charges initially, she was facing only twelve by the time of her trial on May 24, 1431. These related to God directly contacting her and wearing male clothing. Nobody knows truly the extent of her interrogation and ill treatment. It is also unknown if Joan, who was illiterate, knew what she was signing when she made her mark on the confession. What was recorded is that she confessed her supposed sins, promising not to wear men's clothing in exchange for life imprisonment. We do not have records of what went on during those next few days. However, she put back on her male attire and told her judges the voices had reappeared. Angry, her accusers revoked her life sentence and planned her execution for May 30, 1431.

> I would rather die than do something which I know to be a sin, or to be against God's will.
>
> —Joan of Arc

She was sentenced to death to be burned at the stake. She was nineteen years old. Guards shaved her head before the execution. Facing death, she was a gratified and valiant Warrior Mother. She rebirthed her nation and restored its sovereignty. The people of France were her children. She was brave, still, and silent while the flames engulfed her body with tears streaming down her face. In her final words, she affirmed, "Jesus, Jesus, Jesus!"

> Children say that people are hung sometimes for speaking the truth.
>
> —Joan of Arc

Joan's brothers and supporters successfully petitioned Pope Callixtus III for a retrial, and twenty-five years later the church restored her good name. Posthumously, a new unbiased court declared her innocent of all charges, and her verdict was overturned July 7, 1456. Declared a martyr in the church's ruling, she was judged wrongly executed by unethical clergy. They proved her opponents were using a church trial for nonspiritual political purposes. She would have been forty-four years old at that time had her life been spared. After she was declared venerable by Pope Leo the 13th on January 27, 1894, and officially beatified by Pope Pius the 10th on April 11, 1909, the Catholic Church finally completed a long process to canonize her St. Joan of Arc by Pope Benedict May 15, 1920. While her feast day is celebrated on May 30, her birthday on January 6, the feast of the Epiphany in the Catholic Church, has come to be celebrated as well. This Warrior Mother and patron saint of France is an enduring symbol of French unity and patriotism.

As a youngster, my reflection on Joan of Arc was my first contemplation on sovereignty. To be governed by our rightful ruler was both historically and contemporarily relevant during our civil rights struggles of the '60s. Sovereignty implies that *all* citizens are served by our public servants and protected from domination both from outsiders of the nation and discrimination within. Secondarily, it means to me that citizens are supported and empowered with camaraderie from a shared national pride and solidarity. Joan of Arc went from victory to betrayal. Though she regained territory for her nation and established a rightful heir to France's leadership, she was not supported when the tide turned against her, and she became a living sacrifice to her cause. In my life, it was Rosa Parks, Malcom X, Martin Luther King Jr. and countless others who were fighting for sovereignty for all citizens. It was Martin Luther King Jr., Malcolm X, and many others who became the human sacrifice.

I have lived long enough to see the cycles of progress and pushback repeated over and over again. Like Joan, we can get weary of the battle and be tricked or confused for a short period of time to give in to our oppressors. But we also can rally to face injustice with courage and conviction with a righteous indignation that focuses our energies on uplifting ourselves, our families, and our communities, despite man's inhumanity to man. We must acknowledge and confront the evil of racism and sexism and every social injustice to build a sovereign nation and a peaceful world for all.

This Warrior Mother has taught me honor. There is no time like the present to follow our calling. All time is now. Others have a right to be, feel, and believe what they desire or what they have been programed to believe. When others' beliefs interfere with the freedoms we all should enjoy, these beliefs need to be addressed. Being true to ourselves is the ultimate courage, when all around us are doubters.

My Daughter Afryea's Stepmother

My Daughter Afryea's Stepmother

I divorced my children's father when my youngest daughter, Afryea, was just a toddler. It was not until she turned nine years old that her father requested visitation rights. Prior to our divorce when we were separated, his visitation was supervised because of his alcoholism and the civil protection order that followed the domestic violence incident. I had moved on with my life in those years and remarried, and my daughter was her stepfather's little girl. I resisted visitation at first but agreed to meet with my ex-husband and his new wife.

It was hard to tell if my ex-husband was in recovery because he tended to be a binge drinker in the first place. He could have long periods of sobriety and normalcy followed by drunkenness. This could vary from being the gregarious life of the party, the weeping, "Please forgive me, I'm so sorry" tragic state, or the verbal abuse that finally deteriorated to the shock and awe that led to our divorce. The first period of normalcy lasted through the first nine years of our happy marriage prior to his estranged mother, who was an alcoholic, passing. Then the roller coaster of our life began. My daughter was born during happy times when I believed sobriety might be his new life choice. It had not lasted long after.

I liked his new wife. She had two children of her own, a son the same age as our daughter, and a little girl six years younger. She was a caring person. She was responsible and down to earth. We talked candidly. She was a devoted Muslim from Morocco. She was pleasant, kind, and generous. She had a faith, trust, and optimism I appreciated. She was no pushover. She had strong opinions and beliefs, and being dominated or mistreated by a man was not one of them. Maybe that is why she left her country to move here to the United States to give her children and especially her daughter an opportunity for a different life. I too had seen the vast potential in my ex-husband. I was hoping he could turn things around. I wished the best for them.

We thought a lot alike, sharing similar values, and developed a friendship. Her husband, my ex, complained frequently that we were "ganging up on him." She assured me that she would take care of my little girl the same way she would take care of her own children. I arranged my daughter's visitation with her and not my ex-husband. It was working out well. I did not hear much from my daughter about what went on at her father's house. I did not demand to know. I let her know the door was open to discuss it. She never did. She did stop visiting, however, when her stepmother and father separated and then later divorced. When my daughter was in Rio de Janeiro, Brazil, as a foreign exchange student for her senior year of high school we were working on her college applications, and she sent me the following story as an answer to a question about her real-life hero. And the story goes:

> My parents divorced when I was toddler. I didn't remember my biological father in either a bad or good way. Before I started visiting him at the age of nine, my mother told me in a serious voice, "Your father has a disease. He is an alcoholic." I immediately shut down; I did not want to hear more. My imagination had created a father with no faults. My mom was already destroying my perfect perception of him.
>
> My mother formed a friendship with my stepmother, so she knew she would take care of me. One day my father tried to take me to the store after he had been drinking. I immediately went to my stepmom for help. I knew he was in no shape to drive. She immediately intervened for my safety. I knew that although my father wanted to, he was unable to looking out for my

> best interest. My stepmother suffered ill treatment from my dad whenever she protected me, but she always did. She saved my life that day and showed amazing courage. I learned selflessness from her. I now speak up for those who can't or are too scared to, whenever I have the opportunity.

That is why she is my Warrior Mother. She became the warrior for me when I needed her to step up for my child. She is inspiring. Her perseverance teaches me to stand up for myself and courageously stand up for others. Her support blessed me in expected and unexpected ways.

Warriors can come like a victor on a white horse for the battles of our lives, and she was that for me. We were real in each other's lives. We didn't have a history, and we do not have a future. We had an intersection of our lives, and she kept her promise. She promised she would be there for me with my daughter, our daughter. What a blessing!

In the last conversation I had with this Warrior Mother, she was fighting for her life and her kids' lives. She was telling me her troubles with her husband. He was accusing her of just using him to get citizenship to this country. She wanted a separation. I acknowledged I was not the most objective person she should discuss this with and reminded her that I left him before she even married him. I also saw his potential, his charm, and his good side. But when it is bad, it is really bad, and nobody has to live with that stress when their mate is not even trying to get help, when he does not even acknowledge there is a problem. I think she wanted my approval, my permission, or maybe she was just letting me know she would be standing down her guard, her tour of duty over. After her stepmother left her father, my daughter only visited him with me present. It was my tour of duty now!

Chapter 10

Grandmother Mother

Grandmother Mother intergenerational and mothering her adult children and her children's children. She has straddled the generations between her children and her aging parents and has become proficient in planning and organizing. She knows her limitations. She knows how to get the help she needs. She does not overdo it. Her role is to pass the baton to the next generation. She is good at time management and can help us develop our own system by realizing our strengths and challenges.

It is okay not be able to do it all. It is no problem to get help when needed. There is no shame in not being all things to all people or the go-to person. There is no disgrace and even a benefit to be more efficient by asking others for help. Grandmother Mother also realizes that we have to take time to train and communicate with persons assisting us to give them the direction they need. Yet she is wise enough to consider alternatives that have developed more recently if they are more beneficial.

The argument I hear from women is it is easier to do it themselves then to argue, encourage, or coerce other family members or children to help them with activities required for the smooth functioning of the entire family. There still seems to be an expectation in the mind of society that with women's liberation we are meant to the superwomen, like the 1980s advertisement for Enjoli: "I can bring home the bacon, stir it up in a pan, and never let you forget you're a man!" Grandmother Mother will assure us this is garbage and make sure our priority is taking care of ourselves first so we can take care of others!

> Many hands make light work.
>
> —African proverb

True liberation is knowing we are in this together and share responsibilities. Taking the time to pass the torch ensures continuity. It is also important to cultivate sharing of knowledge and information from youth to their elders. Taking time to help our elders assists our youth with the development of patience.

My friend Dr. Lisa Merritt, with the Multicultural Health Institute in Sarasota, Florida, has many wonderful programs, but the Positive Aging and Wellness Series speaks to this process. Each monthly event includes both a wellness section and a technology session. Elders can bring their phones, laptops, etc., and any technology questions, and they are educated by youth in the community. They also are educated by experts on health and wellness topics to assist in healthy Aging. The York County Agency on Aging has a Rent-a-Kid program for elders sixty years or older. The teenagers make a little extra income while being of service to their elders doing the heavy work around the yard and house. I encourage elders who are overdoing it physically to get the assistance of young people. Frequently elders are reluctant to take to help. It is a win-win situation because the elders need physical assistance and the young people need elderly guidance. Often when their parents are talking to them, teenagers hear "blah, blah. blah, blah, blah, blah," but they hear the same information from an elder outside of their normal circle and a light bulb goes off. These teenagers have an opportunity to interact with seniors who have wisdom to share. We need to create more efforts like these within our communities to improve sharing between the ages.

Grandma Moses

Grandma Moses

Grandma Moses's Journey

> Life is what we make it, always has been, always will be.
>
> —Grandma Moses

I am drawn to the life of Grandma Moses because she never gave up. She teaches us resiliency. She was able to continue to create and recreate herself as the conditions around her and her life changed. As I approach the age of retirement, I am not looking forward to doing nothing and withering away as I age. I am looking forward to a new beginning where I can use the experience and perceptions from my career to share with others in an even more meaningful and profound way.

Grandma Moses's Journey

> I was happy and contented, I knew nothing better and made the best out of what life offered.
>
> —Grandma Moses

Grandma Moses proves there is life after childrearing, as one of the most famous US painters starting in her seventies. She was born Anna Mary Robertson, the third of ten children, to poor farmers. She was hired out to help another family to do housework at the age of twelve to help support the family income. She was hardworking as a child. Her schooling was very limited in a one-room country school. She married another hired worker, Thomas Salmon Moses, in her twenties. They moved to Virginia, rented a farm, and worked the land. Of the ten children she gave birth to, five died as babies. A mother, wife, farmer, and entrepreneur, she sold butter and potato chips to her neighbors. She had four grown children before she started her amazing painting career.

> Painting's not important. The important thing is keeping busy.
>
> —Grandma Moses

Mother Moses enjoyed needlework, sewing, and embroidering. A hard worker all her life, she never considered being idle. Crippling arthritis in her hands caused her to take up painting. When her hands could not hold a needle any more, she decided on a paint brush. She painted for the sheer love of the art. She was a self-taught artist. Her work would be classified as folk art. Resourceful, she made her first painting using house paints made out grape juice or lemon juice. She started painting seriously in her late seventies.

> If I had not started painting, I would have raised chickens.
>
> —Grandma Moses

Her studio was an old kitchen table in the utility room. In her tattered swivel chair resting on two large pillows, she would paint for five to six hours a day. She would sit quietly reminiscing, and once she captured the image, "Then I'll get an inspiration and start painting; then I'll forget everything, everything except how things used to be and how to paint it so people will know how we used to live." She enjoyed the beginning of her sessions because she was "steadier" and her hands fresher. Her painting strategy: First the sky, then the mountains, then the hills, then the trees, then the houses, then the cattle and then the people. Her tiny figures were halted in action and cast no shadows.

> What a strange thing is memory, and hope; one looks backward, the other forward; one is of today, the other of tomorrow. Memory is history recorded in our brain, memory is a painter, it paints pictures of the past and of the day.
>
> —Grandma Moses

She painted with the vivid color, action, and humor of her life, depicting scenes from her window, county fairs, and farm activities, such as making soap, apple butter, maple syrup, and candles. She painted scenes from fond memories of her early life. She painted true to herself with a childlike joy, naïveté, and love. Her work was described as lighthearted and optimistic, fresh, and adorable, showing the world as beautiful and good.

> A primitive artist is an amateur whose work sells.
>
> —Grandma Moses

She was discovered in 1938. She was selling her paintings in the country store for five dollars. The art dealer wanted more and went to her home. In order to provide the ten pictures promised, she cut one in half because she only had nine. She was a tiny, lively, cheerful, and charming, with a quick wit and mischievous eyes. She would give a stern look to a misbehaving child and playful sarcasm to her admirers. She was keenly observant of all that was going on around her. Reflecting at ninety-five years old she sensed how things were changing and moving faster. She felt people were more satisfied with life when there was less things, less worry, less anxiety and more contentment, more happiness, more laughter.

> If people want to make a fuss over me, I let 'em, but I was the same person before as I am now.
>
> —Grandma Moses

She charmed spectators with her honesty and simplicity in her first exhibit in New York. She was unassuming and down to earth. She has had multiple one-man shows abroad, touring Europe for two years. Her children's story book illustrating forty-seven reproductions of her painting sold over twenty thousand copies before it was even published.

> I look back on my life a good days work, it was done and I am satisfied with it. I made the best out of what life offered.
>
> —Grandma Moses

After spending many years struggling and in poverty, she enjoyed remarkable success. By the age of eighty, paintings that first sold for five dollars later were sold for $8,000 to $10,000. Her fame, pain, and age did not stop her production rate. During her life, she painted over one thousand pictures. She was honored by governors and presidents. Grandma Moses Day was proclaimed in New York City on her hundredth and hundred and first birthdays. She produced twenty-five paintings after her hundredth birthday. She lived and worked joyfully until her body was reported to have just worn out. She died at the age of 101. Her estimated earnings reached nearly $500,000.

> Now that I am ninety-five years old, looking back over the years, I have seen many changes taking place, so many inventions have been made. Things now go faster. In olden times things were not so rushed. I think people were more content, more satisfied with life than they are today. You don't hear nearly as much

> laughter and shouting as you did in my day, and what was fun for us wouldn't be fun now. … In this age I don't think people are as happy, they are worried. They're too anxious to get ahead of their neighbors, they are striving and striving to get something better. I do think in a way that they have too much now. We did with much less.
>
> —Grandma Moses

There is a detail and a persistence, an organization and a structure in every stroke as you create a piece of art, the drawings for this book, and the words on each page. Grandmother Mother teaches us this perseverance. I started the mother's drawings initially to avoid copyright infringement but quickly realized it was more than that. It was to make a deeper connection to all my Mothers' Council. My artwork has been special to me since childhood—a self-expression that is close to my heart. The images I created while writing this book have become very personal to me. It brought the spirit of these wonderful mothers into my aura to tell their stories and for me to tell mine.

> It was sixth grade when I realized that my art could have an effect on other people.
>
> —Deborah Bernal

Growing up in Painesville, Ohio, as part of a small, close-knit immigrant Jamaican community, was strained in the 1960s in America. The small black community didn't quite accept us. The white community generally rejected us. It didn't help that our parents were struggling to get us a good education and put us in Catholic school against our will. My sisters and I were the only blacks in a school from kindergarten through the eighth grade. My brother Patrick had already graduated from St. Mary's Elementary School. It was the time of civil rights struggle and the black power movement. My brother left Painesville a clean-cut gentleman, graduate of Cathedral Latin High School, and in 1968 came back from college at Ohio State a revolutionary. With his afro, goatee, and mustache, he looked like a black youth I would see on the nightly news at a protest rally. My parents weren't pleased, but I liked it. I couldn't wait to get to college myself!

I was twelve years old in sixth grade. In my school, religion and art class were together. As we learned our Catechism lessons we got to draw. I loved drawing. I was a doodler. There were always images in my head from my dreams that I couldn't wait to get on paper. This day we were asked to draw our favorite Bible story. I knew immediately what I wanted to draw—the woman being healed by touching the hem of Jesus's garment. Her faith had healed her. I went to work.

Of course, my brother would be Jesus. After all, the nuns told me that Michelangelo used his relatives to paint the ceiling of the Sistine chapel, so I would use my family. His friends Walter and Dennis would be the disciples. One of the disciples was very dark. I made him almost black as night. One was "high yellow," as we called it, and I made my brother caramel brown even though he and I were considered light skinned. I took creative license and gave him a tan. After all, there were only so many colors in the Crayola box. I was pleased. It turned out beautifully. So imagine my surprise when Sister Mary Catherine called me to her desk to explain my picture. Then she took me to the principal's office! I did not understand how I ended up in the principal's office this time. It was not like the last time when I was teased by being called tar baby in the playground by an Italian little boy darker than me. Or when my classmate insulted me when she said that she wished she was black so she did not have to take a bath. "Who told you to draw this?" the head mother queried. "She did," I responded, looking at Sister Mary Catherine. "I didn't!" she insisted! They were perplexed. And so was I.

Next thing I knew they had called my parents to arrange a home visit. I told my parents what happened at the dinner table that evening. I think they expected to see my family dressed in fatigues with berets and machine guns like their image of the Black Panther Party. But when the nun arrived, she did find Jamaican art on the walls all over the home, with black people and native art. The white Jesus picture they gave my mom on Palm Sunday was still with the dried palms above her bedroom dresser mirror. They didn't get to see that. They kept inquiring about the picture I had drawn in vague terms, trying to get my parents to express some shock or concern about the content, but they had nothing but glowing accolades for my budding artistry. My parents knew what that nun was driving at but never gave her the satisfaction. They commented on how talented an artist I was and how proud they were of me and what a beautiful picture it was. She never got what she came for, someone in my own family to discredit my portrayal. She never gave the picture to my parents. Who knows what became of it. The nun left just as confused as she arrived, unsatisfied because no one in my house had problems with me drawing a black Jesus. And how could the Nuns speak up? They would be too embarrassed to bring it up. It would be politically incorrect and morally incorrect after they made us memorize our catechism, "We are made in the image and likeness of God"!

Mama Edra Derricks

Mama Edra Derricks

I NEEDED A GRANDMOTHER. I, like my other siblings, left home to go to college and ended up a transplant. Nobody stayed local from my family. I remained in DC since undergrad. Married with two stepchildren and a two-year-old and traveling back and forth to Baltimore during my residency, a grandma's unconditional love was what I needed and what I found in Mama Edra Derricks. My son was ready to start preschool. We enrolled him at an independent African-centered school, and I was greeted at the door by an elder I recognized from our church, St. Augustine's, the Mother Church of African-American Catholics in the nation's capital. She gave me, my husband, and my son great big hugs and kisses as she opened the door that morning and every morning, and she did it for everyone!

We loved her hugs and kisses, and she hugged and kissed everybody, every time she saw them. You could not get away from the door without getting her hug and kiss when dropping off or picking up your children. She scolded us adults for not having a coat on in inclement weather while rushing from the car to the school to drop our kids off. Dropping off our children at school was like dropping them off at grandma's house. It was a beautiful way to start the day.

She lived directly across the street from the school and worked before and aftercare. She kept candy in her house and gave it out. Children from the school and the neighborhood came over to the house for the candy, and she shared her sweetness with them as well.

On weekends coming to the school for an early program, I was often the first to arrive. She had the keys to the building. It was never too early to knock on the door to ask for the keys because she was always up. She was an early riser. Sometimes she would have already walked miles to the store and back those mornings before I arrived. She loved to sit and talk, share ideas, and give advice.

A word to the wise is sufficient.

She had long philosophical discussions about education, home ownership, and parenting. She always expressed that education is critical. She emphasized that children have to be intensely supported by their parents giving them the opportunity to expand their knowledge. She encouraged us to let our daughter travel without us abroad from an early age with People to People Ambassador Program to Australia and China. She always came to support her when she did programs for the community about her experiences on her trips. She believed everyone should be learning something every day. There is always something each of us can learn. She was always inspired by the children because they were ready learners, admiring their openness, innocence, and unchecked response to new information.

She was the youngest of three and the only girl. Her mother passed shortly after she was born. When she was about four years old, she and her brothers were placed in boarding school. She went to Rock Castle, Bensalem, Pennsylvania, founded in 1899 and run by the Sisters of the Blessed Sacrament for Indians and Colored People. This order of nuns was founded by now canonized Saint Katharine Drexel, who was superior general and opened many schools. Mama Derricks reported that the nuns firmly disciplined the children. She stayed there until the age of sixteen years, when she refused to return and came back to live with her father in their family home in DC.

There she went to Cardoza High School, then Minors Teachers College, majoring in English grammar. She never did graduate but was a stickler about grammar all her life, constantly correcting all in her earshot. She remained passionate about education and was involved with the education of students all of her life.

She worked as an elevator operator and got married, and together they had nine children. They had a home heated with a coal-burning stove. The coal was hard to come by, and often they were cold by morning. She held a variety of jobs over the years, including working in a bakery and as a telephone operator. She worked as a char woman in offices. This Grandmother Mother worked at many educational institutions and used her influence to inspire students. She worked at Bertie Backus Middle School for the math and science departments doing office work. She worked as an assistant at St. Augustine's School and Church. She worked as a teacher at St. Augustine, Bertie Backus Middle School, as well as Holy Name.

Count your blessings.

A lifelong member of St. Augustine's Church, Mama Derricks was a volunteer to take the children camping and on retreats and would love to cook for these groups. A devout Catholic, she was also very spiritual. As an optimist, she encourages gratitude and to never regret. She always said, "Count your blessings!" She prayed nightly prayers for everybody. She remained watchful and prayerful over family, neighbors, and all the people and organizations she loved and worked with. She loved to pray her rosary. She took food to the homeless on a regular basis. She was compassionate. Never selfish, she was continuously giving, caring, and sharing—a true child of God!

She married Mr. Horace Derricks in the late '70s. He was a good man with a lot of children. The two families joined as one, and everyone got along well. She had an amicable relationship with her stepchildren's mother. Mama Derricks was helpful to me as I was going through my divorce. She had known my husband from our church and the school. She, like everyone at St. Augustine's Church, was surprised at our divorcing. We had presented at family and adult spiritual retreats, met with the pope as representatives of the parish, and had been the lead couple for the marriage encounter group. People thought we were the ideal couple, but little did they know that things could change so quickly. It seemed as if after his mother's death, he went overnight from a model husband and father to a binge alcoholic.

Don't do anything I wouldn't do.

Mama Derricks could sympathize. She had found love and happiness in her second marriage. She gave me hope and encouragement during my courtship and remarriage. She gave me good advice on getting along with the ex, my ex-in-laws, or "outlaws" as I called them jokingly, and how to be a good, easygoing ex-wife and co-parent with prayer for but no expectations of my ex-husband's changing. Just dealing with the reality of who people have shown you they are and praying for their highest good and greatest joy.

It was Mama Derricks who always reminded me to put the children first and swallow any false pride I might have or even righteous indignation to never allow a negative word to be uttered in front of the children related to their dad. Keeping this rule, she suggested, bought me the time to get grounded again. She was a stabilizing force in our family life, and I could look forward to her smiling face, encouraging words, hugs, and kisses each school day morning and aftercare night. I went to my psychiatrist and my monthly prayer rituals and continued my weekly divorce counselling that year with the priest to return to a point of forgiveness, healing, and love.

Better to be seen and not heard.

As a mother of nine, she was very strict and organized. The children were not allowed out after dark. She worked a lot of night hours, and the older siblings cared for the younger ones. She was organized and a hard worker, and chores were not a chore to her. She wanted to get it done. It was never a problem. She was physically a strong woman from years of hard work. She had biceps as big as a man's from insisting on getting on her hands and knees scrubbing floors. She could jump double-dutch jump rope into her eighties like a youth. She was a walker and never drove. She took the bus, got a ride, or walked. She would walk from her home to my office and back three miles each way or to the church one and a half miles each way. She walked to the grocery store a mile away. She was adamant about walking daily. She walked miles a day all over town.

She moved back in the family home when her father fell ill to take care of him. She lost her father in 1996. She loved to cook and opened her home to family and friends, regularly entertaining. Mama Derricks loved to tell jokes, some rather risqué. She kept a lot of jokes in her head and many not for young ears. She never let the children hear them. She accumulated them over the years and had a great memory. She loved people, and she liked to make them laugh. She enjoyed playful banter. Every Sunday she had open houses. Starting the cooking on Saturday and on Sunday morning on the way to church Mass, she would leave the homemade rolls to rise. She was organized and had a system and a plan. She was always supportive of her children. She loved to sit and talk to her grandchildren and give advice. She loved the holidays. She would cook and hosted the entire family at her home.

As an advocate and social activist, she was blunt, up front, and straight ahead! She would stand up, speak up, and speak out about anything and everything she found wrong, and she didn't hesitate to speak to anybody! She did not allow any foul language, inappropriate activities around the children, or misconduct around the school. This Grandmother Mother would confront neighbors and passersby as well, known or unknown, fearlessly! She would challenge them verbally and shake her index finger at them. She would correct any person, anywhere in the city, even strangers at the bus stop, for misbehavior. She would not allow the children to act inappropriately. Knowing right from wrong, Mama Derricks made sure we knew, and that she knew we knew, and this made us accountable.

She was well known downtown in DC government. She would walk downtown to see what was going on and get involved. She worked at the police station, with city council, and with the mayor's office. They all knew her and were accountable to this Grandmother Mother for their behavior. On the election committee, she worked at the polls. As an election board captain, she was passionate about the sacrifices blacks made to vote and the obligation we have to our ancestors to honor their memory by exercising our civic responsibility to vote. She was active in the Advisory Neighborhood Commission (ANC) and was elected by her ward as an ANC commissioner. She passionately voiced protests when there was a need to do so, and she was very aware and assertive to the needs of the people.

As an activist involved in the protests movements over the years, she would be on-site speaking out for positive change. She could be very passionate and appropriately aggressive. She was not shy and would not hold her tongue. She was on the verge of being arrested for protesting the neighborhood bank on Georgia Avenue. The neighbors rallied under her leadership and support against discriminatory practices and predatory lending, almost closing down that bank branch.

It was not only important to her that she own her own home, but she also encouraged her community members. She worked for many years and played a major role in DC with the ACORN movement and did good work. The Association of Community Organizations for Reform Now (ACORN) was the nation's largest community organization of low- and moderate-income families, working together for social justice and stronger communities from the 1970s to 2010. ACORN's accomplishments included successful campaigns for better housing, schools, neighborhood safety, health care, job conditions, and more. Mama Derricks' work with ACORN was in complete integrity, and she avoided the scandal that occurred that led to the organization's demise.

Mama Derricks loved to have people over and entertain. She loved her home, food, and laughing. She would watch the neighborhood through the kitchen window. She became part of the Neighborhood Senior Watch. From her exemplary work on the Neighborhood Watch Patrol, she was recruited by the police department to become one of the first in DC senior police officer from a recommendation of her local councilmen. She enjoyed senior policing working with the youth. She did sharpshooter training and was a good shot, gloating over her target bullseye. She had open houses for the local police department, which was right on her block.

Mama Derricks worked in before and after care for the school for over twenty-five years. She loved the drums at the school and the Yoruba temple. She enjoyed the African ceremonies. She and Baba Oriafo, an esteemed male role model and mentor, enjoyed our collective expressions of appreciation for them as elders. After she was widowed, we tried to hook her up with Baba Oriafo. She responded, laughing, “I don’t want any old man. No old man can keep up with me!”

Pray for me because I pray for you.

She started at the school when my son Hasani arrived in 1985. My daughter’s term at the school started thirteen years later at the age of four. Mama Derricks was there through her middle school graduation in 2008. She had health issues in 2008, and many thought her career was finished, but she came back after a year or so and was able to return to working at the school for six or nine months before she passed.

Her life was busy and fulfilling. She was very thoughtful and giving. She was blessed and had no worries at her time of rest. She peacefully passed away on Friday, December 28, 2012, at the age of ninety-three, leaving her nine children, thirty-six grandchildren, seventy-three great-grandchildren, eighteen great-great-grandchildren, and a host of other relatives and friends to carry on in her behalf. St. Augustine’s was overflowing with well-wishers from all walks of life at her funeral, a testament to a life well lived. Councilman Jim Graham gave her a citation and proclaimed the day Edra Derricks Day in Washington, DC. She died with the full honor of the police department with a police honor guard at her burial at Mount Olivet Cemetery.

Being overburdened slows us down, weakens us, and can grind our progress to a halt, and then our bodies just give out on us. We, by ourselves, will never get it done, and humanity will never be finished. We will always be looking ahead to the next goal or next accomplishment. We are creators, and our process never ends. Our minds move much more swiftly than our bodies can manifest. This Grandmother Mother Mama Derricks is our role model for collective work and responsibility. We need to expand our resources by working with one another. She charges us with her legacy to be and do for our family, community, nation, and race all we can to be: persons of good moral character to right social injustice and to leave a legacy of love, hard work, and joyful play.

Chapter 11

QUEEN MOTHER

A Queen Mother is a leader. A Queen Mother is directed in her role with others by her spiritual vision. She acts as a spiritual messenger for the community, leading to our self-discovery. Queen Mothers become pure, unconditioned channels that show us our undiscovered potential. They espouse wisdom and trustworthy intuition. It is the destiny of all of our relationships to become holy. Our Queen Mother is our role model for that potential within us. When we bring this purity to our relationships, we are striving to become holy.

Ask for Guidance from a Place of Wisdom before I Act

Queen Mother gives us courage to follow God's commands by being an example of trust and full obedience. She properly uses her words and authority cheerfully, positively, and wisely. In ancient times, the Queen Mother selected from her sons the future leader for the people. Not birth order but divine order led by her inner spiritual voice. A Queen Mother could be a great orator, so people traveled far and wide to hear her speak or a discreet guide that gives personal messages individually and quietly. By either method, she is a spiritual messenger. She lifts the spirits of the faithful. She possesses a wonderful influence and a delightful attitude with an unwavering commitment that encourage these qualities in others.

Deborah the Prophetess

Deborah the Prophetess

Queen Mother Deborah, the Biblical Mother of Israel

SHE WAS ORDAINED BY GOD with the spiritual power of discernment to ensure God's will, not man's will, be done.

Little is known of this biblical figure's birth and life. Though we do know that this charismatic leader was married to Lappidoth—"Now Deborah, the wife of Lappidoth, was a prophetess. She judged Israel at that time" (Judges 4:4 MEV)—we do not know if they had any biological children. She was a prophetess during these times when the prophets were the intercessors between God and the people of Israel. This gift of divinely inspired knowledge of God's will was a high spiritual calling and held that person, man or woman, in high esteem in the society. They sought out her just and righteous wisdom as judge, negotiator, and counselor. This matriarch is one of only six female prophetesses recorded in the Bible.

Respectful and Respected, Inspiring Others to Come to Her for Her Judgment and Counsel

One of the wisest of Old Testament women, Deborah became the leader of the Israelites' at a time not known for female leadership. She became known as the "mother of Israel" for her life of service to her country. She held court and settled disputes for her people at "The Palm of Deborah." "She would sit under the palm tree of Deborah between Ramah and Bethel in the hill country of Ephraim. The children of Israel would go up to her for her to render judgment" (Judges 4:5 MEV). Palm trees were rare in Palestine, and therefore that location became her landmark. Faithful to God, she lived in integrity and in her devotion to God's will. She deciphered the revelations of

God's will and was filled with God's grace. She was instructed by God's command, and the responsibility to uplift the entire Hebrew nation rested on her shoulders.

Living a Life of Purpose for Family, Community, Nation, and Faith

After losing their ruler, Ehud, and becoming disobedient to God's law, the Israelites had lost control of their territory for the last twenty years. It was a time of chaos when their nation was oppressed by outside rulers, the Canaanites, and Deborah's people had fallen into spiritual decline and corruption. Deborah had the power of sound judgment and profound thinking and used her powers of persuasion to restore her people's loyalty to God. The Canaanites were ruled by King Jabin and protected by the general Sisera, the army's commander. His troops were a mighty force of nine hundred chariots fitted with iron. These were the most powerful tools of war during ancient times, and that struck horror into the hearts of foot soldiers only armed with swords.

The Jewish people prayed for relief. Their prayers were answered through the prophet Deborah, who called for Barak to advise him of God's will for him and his people.

> She sent for Barak son of Abinoam from Kedesh in Naphtali and said to him, "The Lord God of Israel commands you, 'Go and deploy troops at Mount Tabor, and take ten thousand men from the tribes of Naphtali and Zebulun with you. I will draw Sisera, the commander of the army of Jabin, with his chariots and large army to you at the River Kishon and give him into your hands." (Judges 4:6–7 MEV)

But Barak was unwilling without her coming along with him. She courageously agreed to go with him to battle as he requested. It was imperative to follow God's commands. She was willing to lead by being an example of trust and full obedience. Because of his lack of faith, she revealed that he would not be the death of Sisera. This honor would be granted to a woman.

The mission was to confront oppression to correct wrongs and restore national sovereignty, sanctity, and security.

Her prophecy had stirred up hope in her oppressed people, and their faith in her guidance and leadership gave them the determination to take action. They went to Mt. Tabor as she commanded. When the victory was upon them, she spoke to Barak, reminding him of the promise of God to give him the expectation of the victory that lay ahead. "Then Deborah said to Barak, 'Get up, for this is the day that the Lord has given Sisera into your hands. Has not the Lord gone out before you?' So Barak went down from Mount Tabor with ten thousand men behind him" (Judges 4:14 MEV). He took the army as commander and confronted the Canaanite army. Then, as vowed, Sisera's army fell to the army of Barak by the sword, despite their heavy military advantage. Sisera fled on foot, abandoning his chariot. His entire army was killed. Barak then pursued the commander Sisera.

Another prophecy fulfilled

Meanwhile Sisera had sought refuge in what he had thought was a safe haven. The woman there, Jael, brought him into her tent, covered him with blankets, and gave him milk to drink. As he laid down to rest, he asked her to stand guard in the doorway to divert anyone in search of him. Exhausted, he laid fast asleep, and Jael took a tent peg and hammer and drove it through his temple and into the ground. It was then that Jael went to meet Barak and showed him to her tent to witness Sisera's dead body. His death at this woman's hand fulfilled Deborah's prophesy. They were able to destroy the stronghold of Jabin, king of Canaan. This gained Deborah respect as the judge, warrior, leader, prophetess, queen, and deliverer of her people.

A Woman of Great Talents and Great Faith, Leading with Innovation and Motivation

She was fifth of a line of leaders in Judges and the only women of the twelve judges. Deborah was a multifaceted figure. In addition to her heroism, she was a writer, poetess, singer, dancer, and songwriter. She sang reassuring war chants and conquest songs inspiring warriors to go into battle. Her "Song of Praise" in Judges 5 (MEV) was a clever reminder to her people of their past disobedience and subjugation, call to victory, and need for gratitude and righteous behavior, also known as the "Song of Deborah." She praises the believers who came forward and rebukes those that did not answer the call to liberation. A strong administrator, she demonstrated the power of womanhood. She remained true to God's word, rulings with equality, righteousness, justice, and mercy. The Jews lived in peace and harmony for forty years under her astute leadership.

What an inspiration this Queen Mother Deborah, my namesake. The name *Deborah* means bee. The bee is one of the most organized of creatures, each member tailor made for their job in the hive. And so was Deborah as queen tailor made for her destiny. What the life of Deborah shows me is that we are all perfectly made for our destiny on this earth during our incarnation on this physical plane. We have the will to choose to step into that destiny, or we can deny it. I look to these stories of faith and courage to give me faith and courage. The call is a voice within our souls. Listening to that still, small voice makes it stronger still. Like strengthening weak muscles, we must use our faith in small ways and grow our faith stronger and stronger to be ready for the bigger and bigger challenges our life has to offer.

Embrace Divine Guidance

Challenges come to us if we do not go out to meet them. We cannot hide from the challenges of life. Life is meant to stretch us. Growth and change are a natural part of life itself. My queens have taught me that it is better to go out and meet the challenges I choose rather than letting fear, stagnation, and distraction choke off my life force and trample my spirit. Like writing this book, developing a wellness program, or working with a mentorship group in the local schools, I seek challenges that stretch me and help others. We can trust ourselves and our intuition, moving forward in faith committed to a process of lifelong learning, or we stay in denial of our issues, thus making the lessons we are learning more frequent and more difficult. Why should we let fear of change, fear of failure, and fear of success keep us spiraling down experiencing our same hard lessons over and over again, getting nowhere fast? Our queens show us that success in life is being the master of ourselves and ruler of our mind and mission. Our faith gives us the strength and courage as our foundation in God's power to intuit it, think it, plan it, feel it, see it, know it, and then do it.

Madame Adji Fatou Seck

Madame Adji Fatou Seck

Our next Queen Mother, Madame Fatou Seck, entered my life at a critical point of crucial decision. Self-centered, egotistical, and arrogant, I had gone through all the stages of death and dying when my husband's alcoholism came to the surface. I tried to ignore it, but it got worse. I tried to explain it away, thinking it was his grieving process. It became more apparent. Angry and whining, I became the martyr, betrayed and abandoned. Begging and pleading, I had no power to make him change or seek help. Depressed and isolated, I felt hopeless. I was suffering in silence, and the secrecy was stifling me. I had to move. I had to get help! Now it was not for him but for myself. My priest suggested Al-Anon. The twelve steps saved me. I came back to myself. It was a time of great spiritual growth for me unlike any other time in my life.

There was an opening in my soul, and now I needed something more. That twelve-step program had been right up my alley. I have always been a self-help junkie, preferring self-help to fiction or any other type of literature. I was on my twelfth step in Al-Anon. I heard of another course from new friends, a young couple I had just met at a family development conference we were attending. They were newlyweds with no children yet but a desire to learn more and be proactive in building their family. By contrast, I was over a decade into what I had thought had been a happy partnership, struggling for my marriage and family life to survive.

When I first met my husband, it was his parenting that I admired most. He was a single father raising two girls, fourteen and nine years old. He cooked, cleaned, and ran the household, getting help from friends and neighbors for special needs of the girls, like their haircare. He wasn't at all shy about discussing their feminine hygiene needs or picking up the products they needed as maturing young girls. I was a medical student riding my bike to school. He was working as a photojournalist for the dental school, riding his bike to work each day. He was trying to surround his girls with good female role models when I got involved in their life. I wanted to be that for them, and later I found I wanted to be more than that. I wanted to be part of the family. When we were married, I became an instant mom of an eleven-year-old and sixteen-year-old. Their brother followed nine months after the wedding. The older children were grown and gone out of the house when the drama started. Our son was only nine years old.

Our son idolized his father. And why wouldn't he? He had been a model father until that time. He cared for him as an infant, while I was in my internship and residency programs. He taught him martial arts, archery, downhill skiing, and snorkeling. They spent a lot of time together watching sports and playing video games. He entertained my son's age mates building forts and making food for their overnights and parties. He was a wonderful cook and took our son on shopping trips to get exotic foods from the markets to make sushi and Indian or Ethiopian foods. He taught our son not only how to cook but how to enjoy eating. We were both sticklers for manners. Our son knew all the silverware for formal meal settings and dined at fancy restaurants from a very young age. We went downhill skiing every other weekend through the winter. We traveled to Jamaica for holidays and retreats a couple times each year, and my son would run through the white sand beaches and dive into the clear blue ocean yelling, "This is the life!" But all this had changed.

My husband and I were alienated. His grief over his mother's death had spiraled into isolation, drunkenness, and now adultery! He was begging for forgiveness and talking like he was willing to change, but I was, needless to say, skeptical. We had not only a home life together but a work life—a family integrative medical practice. He was an alternative practitioner of massage, Wat Su water massage, Thai chi,

chi gong, Tui Na, and traditional Chinese medicine. I combined my practice of nutrition, cleansing and detoxification, yoga, dance, Native American, and African traditional healing and herbs with my holistic allopathic medical practices. Our goal was to have a holistic retreat center. The retreats in Jamaica were our prequel to that plan, but it all seemed to be going up in smoke.

Guided and Directed

This couple told me of classes coming up in Baltimore that they were planning to attend. The subject was deep thought. It sounded like what I needed—contemplation on philosophy to get a connection to make decisions about my future. The course was encouraging, uplifting, and illuminating. From the twelve steps, I had learned about dependence and codependence, surrender and forgiveness. From this course, I focused on my values. True power was coming from the spirit and not forced by the will or imposed by man's law or conditioning through miseducation. Life provides opportunity for evolution of the soul. A beneficial and enlightened life is the goal.

Shift Our Focus onto Life and the Process of Living

Enlightenment requires conscious, consistent effort in deep thought, bringing about understanding and wisdom. We must take time to go within ourselves and ponder the substance of our being. We find all we need and want inside of us. The finding takes effort. The effort can be through logic and reasoning, meditation in silence, prayer or praise, or journaling our gratitude. It can be expressed through the arts: poetry, song, dance, music, literature, and visual art. It can be contacted through nature, rhythm, the revelation of our senses, attunement to the body, and mindfulness. It can be explored through the proverbs, myths, traditions, and rituals of the rich cultural heritage of the many peoples of the earth. While it is an accomplishment to come to serenity within ourselves, it is not enough. We are persons in communion with Mother Earth, humanity, and all creation. It is incumbent on us to "know thyself" but also to uplift humankind. Our thoughts are part of the ocean of human thought. We reflect our inner self in our outer world. Do we like what we see? Are we moving humanity forward? The ancient philosophers put it this way, "I am because we are, and because we are I am." We are all interconnected. We are all our brothers' and sisters' keepers.

Everyone has the right to be valued, honored, and encouraged, the right to wellbeing. We must remain honorable. Fairness requires a win-win-win for the individual, the society, and Mother Earth. Compassion speaks to our receptivity to empathy but not our foolhardy codependence. All are worthy of love and are deserving of respect as they are part of the God force, but it is our responsibility to learn our lessons. No one can do it on our behalf. Compassion gives us the joy and patience to love ourselves through that process and to lovingly stand by others in their process as well.

Balanced Relational Perceptions

Order is a universal constant in natural law and spiritual law. Reciprocity is the capacity to give and receive graciously and gratefully. Balance keeps us humble. It gives us stability when our lessons are trying to throw us off course. It gives us levelheadedness when we are under pressure. It relies not on our thoughts but a belief deep within of the knowledge of our worthiness. When we forget we are worthy, we are out of balance and heading off course. When we know we are out of control and confused, we look to a leader to guide us. It has been said, "When the student is ready the teacher will appear." This is how I came to know Madame Fatou Seck.

A Thirst for Spiritual Knowledge

She was honorable, full of vitality, and strong in God's will. She was a spiritually powerful, humble, yet authoritative leader. She was nearing one hundred years old. Demonstrating the power of eldership and womanhood, inspiring others to come to her for her discernment and thoughtful council, she was actively seeking to help other people. She used holy words with authority. Madame Fatou Seck was cheerful, positive, and wise. This Queen Mother gave us strength and encouragement with a clarity of knowing that could only be divinely inspired. She was a commanding but peaceful force, and people traveled far and wide to be in her presence. She lifted the spirits of the hopeless and made them faithful. She had a magnificent influence and a pleasing attitude with an unwavering commitment to her people—all people. She encouraged these qualities in others. I needed to know more about this noble Queen Mother.

Madame Adji Fatou Seck's Journey

Born 1896 into a family of fishing villagers in Rifisque, Senegal, Adji Fatou Seck had to end her schooling due to ill health. Married by age fifteen, she gave birth to nine children. Her calling as a healer came at age seventeen as she began to treat with herbs and traditional medicines. She was initiated at age twenty-six as an Ndeppkat priestess, an ancient Wolof spiritual tradition of rituals combining the treatment of mental and physical illness. This practice unites almighty God, the ancestors, and the healer with the ailing patient to restore health. It has been proven time and time again since 1946, as Madame Adji Fatou Seck performed over fifty seaside healing rituals, called Coumba Lamba, mandated by and in honor of her spiritual mother, teacher, and leader. She practiced seven days a week due to the high demand for her service, and she still had time to raise her children and preside over a compound of over fifty. It is said that no healing she has undertaken has failed, but she has never claimed to heal anyone. Now Coumba Lamba is one of her birthplaces paramount occurrences.

One of the most celebrated and famous persons in Senegal, Madame Seck was officially recognized by the Senegalese government as a national resource. Her important work has treated and cured thousands. The work is so important that she and her practitioners worked side by side allopathic-trained physicians in hospitals. She regularly worked treating the mentally ill with the psychiatrists at the Fann Hospital in Dakar.

She first ventured out of her homeland to fulfill her sacred duty to perform a Hajj to Mecca in 1959. Then between the September of 1986 and May of 1993, facilitated by Dr. Charles Finch, director of International Health, Morehouse School of Medicine, she made three trips to the United States. Traveling with two assistant priestesses and an interpreter, she met with scholars interested in traditional healing systems and Native American leaders and healers. She met with patrons, mostly African Americans, who heard of her work and traveled far and wide to seek her counsel. She spent time in New York, New Jersey, Philadelphia, Baltimore, Washington DC, and Atlanta. Hundreds came to touch her, see her, and be in her presence. Others of us were lucky enough to get private consultation time with her. I was one of those lucky ones in May of 1993.

Madame Seck had saved the life of her US host with her advice and counsel years before. She had warned her during their meeting in Senegal of three persons trying to do her harm physically and financially. Madame's description allowed her to recognize two of the people right away. She was in a group partnership with two of the individuals, one a man and one a woman. She would later find out that both of them had betrayed her and were stealing money from the business. The third, a young man, was not known to her, but the description was etched in her mind. After all, how else but by divine knowing could this great healer have known of this woman's partners when at that time they had just met and Madame Seck had not been to the US or had never set foot in her office?

Then after Madame Seck's host returned to the United States, she was plunged into intrigue the likes of a 20/20 mystery. A psychotic young man came to the office after hours. He was demanding to get in and pounding on the door looking for her male partner. He relentlessly kept pounding on the door despite being told the office was closed and her partner was not available. He demanded to be let in, and she saw his face through the peep hole. It was the person Madame Seck had described to her months before! She pressed the panic button for the police. Later she would find this young man was manipulated in a plot to kill her for collection of a life insurance policy her male partner had falsified. She and Madame Seck had remained close, and she insisted that I must meet with Madame Seck during this rare occasion.

It was an exceptional opportunity to be in the company of an authentic African tradition healer like Madame Seck, a wellspring of insight, understanding, and experience. She was my Queen Mother here from the motherland, and I came seeking healing. Confused, I wanted things that I thought were not possible. After my residency, I had been trying for six years to have another child. Since we used no birth control, no rhythm method, I thought I'd be pregnant in a couple of years. We hadn't been tested. I had no fertility treatments. It did not happen, and now with my marriage on the rocks, I was sure all my eggs would be dead before I could get a divorce, find a new husband, and get pregnant. I was under tremendous marital and work stress. I did not even know how to frame a question for her when she came in.

The room was dimly lit. Madame Seck's eyes were extremely sensitive to light. She sat down with her interpreter and started, gazing first into my eyes. Her eyes were deep and dark, pleasant but penetrating. Next she gazed into a shallow basket of cowry shells, as she began swirling them around with her hand. She began talking, and I wrote down all she said to me without me saying a word. She answered my thoughts. I would be shown how, I was told, to "let the baby come." She laughed as I thought about my husband. "You have a child with him already!" She was correct. If the marriage worked out, great. If it didn't, oh well—we were already bonded for life through our first child. Would one more make a big difference? Turns out, no! And what of my years of infertility? I was past my mid-thirties! I was told, "Pay attention!" Every step would be revealed to me. It was. Our daughter was born the following April. She is a blessing to our life and a blessing to this world.

When small groups of African Americans began attending the annual Coumba Lamba in Senegal, Madame informed Dr. Charles Finch it was time to do the ceremony on the shores of US soil. The communal healing ceremony was named after Mama Coumba Lamba, the Senegalese "Mother of the Waters," and had been done annually since 1947. She was nearing one hundred years old, and it was the one thing she wanted to do on this earth before she became an ancestor. It was a lot to accomplish, but it occurred in the summer of 1996. The Penn Center for Preservation of Gullah/Sea Island Culture on St. Helena Island, South Carolina, was determined to be the appropriate site for this eight-day ceremony from August 11 to 19. Over six hundred persons attended Coumba Lamba USA with sixty invited guests, staff, or volunteers. The entire event was underwritten by generous contributions as tradition required it be free and open to the public.

I unfortunately did not attend this gathering. I had the baby Madame Adji Fatou Seck and I had spoken of in our consultation, but the marriage had not worked out. I was in the throes of a tumultuous separation required for twelve months if both parties are not in agreement of a divorce. He was not in agreement, but neither was he was willing to move forward to work on the relationship. I wish I had been able to take the opportunity. I know it would have helped my transition, but I was inspired by the reflection I heard from my Earth Mother Sabrina, who had been in attendance.

Sabrina shared about the first day of the ritual. It was clear, and the sky was blue. Not a cloud in sight. The opening rituals had occurred, and a prayer was offered each first night of the ritual for a cleansing of the seekers and the sacred space. Madame Adji Fatou Seck looked to the heavens and started to speak. The Great Mother asked for cooling waters to come and purify the hundreds of seekers present. This Queen Mother's powers were so profound as to be able to influence Mother Nature herself. Within two minutes a drenching downpour of rain washed the crowd as they all stood in awe. They accepted the blessing and dispersed to shelter and rest for the night. Sabrina's experience was one of profound healing and spiritual connection during the eight-day ritual. She had the opportunity to have a one-on-one counsel from Madame Fatou Seck as well, which was enlightening to her life. It was an experience Sabrina will never forget.

Develop My Intuitive Side

My Queen Mother Madame Fatou Seck passed shortly after that ritual, at over one hundred years of age. Prior to being called home to the spirit of the ancestors, she fulfilled her goal of completing the Coumba Lamba USA. Despite leaving the earth plane, she is still hard at work. She is still guiding me in my dreams. During the writing of this book, she came to me in a dream and gave me two acupressure points she told me to press. I asked my husband, who is an acupuncturist, what the energy of the points revealed. These are points of a spiritual gateway between the physical and spiritual that we can use to both ground and open ourselves to spiritual intuition. She continues to show the rich healing traditions of our ancient African holistic spiritual systems. Thank you, Madame, for continuing to bless me.

Chapter 12
Godmother Mother

When our parents select a godmother, they are selecting someone they love and trust to raise their child in case of their demise. They are also choosing a village mother for their child. As adults we choose our Godmother Mother to help us bridge between this physical life and our eternal spiritual life. We are looking for role models and authorities experienced in this life and prepared for the afterlife.

Living with a righteous intention, we define ourselves rather than being defined by the world outside of us. We speak up for ourselves and create our own cosmology. We understand ourselves as a divine manifestation of creation. We realize the essential nature of our being is unconditional love. With this connection to spirit, we feel a deep inner peace that is unshakeable. Nothing coming against us can flourish because we live surrendered to spirit.

Directed to Live in Soul Wisdom, the Knowing with an Open Heart

This Godmother Mother causes us to ask ourselves the big questions but shows us the answer in the way she lives her life. Who am I? Why am I here? Am I really who I profess to be? Am I being all I can be? We are all called to know and speak our own special truth. We realize we are part of a spiritual reality that is beyond our human comprehension, but it is not beyond our intuitive spiritual knowing. As we connect to this spiritual knowing, we can feel it. This Godmother Mother shows us how to find our soul's truth and let it lead our way.

We build reliance on our intuition over our life experience. When you look back at situations and say to ourselves, "I knew that was going to happen!" do not kick yourself! It is not failure. It is a signal that we are becoming more and more aware. It is like building muscles during strength training. We are only able to pick up the next highest weight after doing many repetitions with a lower weight. First we acknowledge the guidance, and finally, we are obedient to the guidance that comes, which opens the channels for more guidance to flow through. Our intuition is strengthened from our trusting, using, and relying on it more and more. With confidence in our spiritual guidance, we become more obedient. By treasuring these intuitive gifts of spirit, we will receive more gifts. Meditation, silencing, and stilling the mind helps us to get connected to this essence of life. Gratitude expands our blessings. I am forever grateful to the ancestral Godmother Mother, Harriet Tubman, and my chosen Godmother Mother, Connie Barber, for the blessing their lives have been for me.

Harriet Tubman

Harriet Tubman

I call her Mother Harriet, and she is my symbol of freedom. She was freed before she ran away from slavery. Her free mind allowed her body to follow the path to her freedom. I heard a person comment that Harriet Tubman lived in Dorchester County, Maryland, which was only about one hundred miles from the Mason-Dixon Line. This person stated, "She did not live so far from the north, so what was the big deal?" I beg to differ. It was a big deal that she risked her life over nineteen times to bring over three hundred slaves to freedom! Slaves were frequently caught in the north and sent back to their southern slave holders. To ensure their freedom, the enslaved runaways initially had to escape all the way to Canada.

> Slavery is the next thing to hell.
>
> —Harriet Tubman

Harriet Tubman was spiritually guided to freedom. She could smell freedom; her senses were keener than the search dogs that were after her. She could have rescued many more. However, they were still imprisoned in their own minds. If it was not such a big deal, why did white slave holders have a $40,000 bounty on her head? That is worth $1.4 million in today's value, and they still could not catch her. She was called Black Moses, and she inspired thousands to seek and find freedom.

> I grew up like a neglected weed, – ignorant of liberty, having no experience of it. Then I was not happy or contented.
>
> —Harriet Tubman

Born in 1822, the fifth child of nine to enslaved parents, Araminta, or "Minty," as she was called, was ordered, with her mother and siblings, to move ten miles away from her father. Her father managed the timber interest of his owner. Her mother, Harriet or "Rit," as she was called, worked in the big house. Minty, from the age of five years old, was forced to care for her younger sibling, as her mother and older siblings were forced to work. She was often hired out to temporary masters. She recalled a brutal mistress who whipped her daily, leaving visible scars. She remembers being forced to work in icy cold winter waters and being neglected, with not enough food or water, making her weak and physically sick. She was often returned as useless after being rented out. Her mother's love and care would heal her, and the cycle of injustice would repeat itself. Three of her sisters were sold to out-of-state buyers, permanently separating their family and requiring two of them to leave their own children behind.

> I said to the Lord, "I'm going to hold steady on to you,
> and I know you will see me through."
>
> —Harriet Tubman

Minty, a young adolescent, accompanied the plantation cook to the local dry goods store to make a purchase. She blocked the path of the overseer who was in the pursuit of a defiant enslaved male child and was nearly killed by a blow to the head from a two-pound iron weight the overseer threw, fracturing her skull. Despite her condition, she was sent back to work in the fields. Harriet Tubman reported years later, "I went to work again and there I worked with the blood and sweat rolling down my face till I couldn't see." Her owner tried to put her up for sale, but there were no buyers for a sick and wounded child suffering from migraines, seizures, and blackouts. Although this caused much pain and suffering, it also gave her a spiritual intuition through dreams, visions, and what she felt was the voice of God speaking directly to her soul, guiding her future course of actions. This spiritual connection was reinforced by her strong African cultural heritage and superimposed evangelical religious teachings required by her slave masters. What was meant to harm her became her supernatural aid.

> … t'wan't *me,* 'twas *de Lord!* I always *tole* him, 'I trust to you., I don't know where to go or what to do, but I expect you to lead me,' an' he always did.
>
> —Harriet Tubman

Deeply spiritual and after a lengthy recovery nurtured by family and friends, she was able to survive her darkest days. Harriet Tubman's physical strength and endurance was enhanced by work in the fields, docks, and timber yards. She had been sent back home and was working under her father when she was able to learn of secret communication networks provided by the black mariners along the Chesapeake Bay. They knew the safe havens and the danger zones and were able to share while working out of earshot of watchful slave holders. She practiced skills of disguise and deception. These, combined with her intuitive knowledge, were the recipe that led to her eventual escape. At twenty-two years old, Harriet had married an older free black man, John Tubman. He forfeited his rights as a husband and a father by marrying an enslaved woman. But five years later, when Harriet's slave owner died, she knew she was about to be sold away from her husband and family. She fled north to freedom without her husband. She listened to her inner voice and was led to her victory.

> When I found I had crossed that line, I looked at my hands to see if I was the same person. There was such a glory over everything; the sun came like gold through trees, and over the fields, and I felt like I was in Heaven.
>
> —Harriet Tubman

Harriet Tubman was tempted by her newfound freedom to stay in its safe and secure embrace. However, she knew she had obtained this gift of freedom, not just for herself; she knew that she must return for her family. She knew she had to go back.

> I had crossed the line. I was free; but there was no one to welcome me to the land of freedom. I was a stranger in a strange land; and my home after all, was down in Maryland; because my father, my mother, my brothers, and sisters, and friends were there. But I was free, and they should be free.
>
> —Harriet Tubman

She said, "I venture only where God send." When she returned for her husband, he had married a free woman and had started a family. Brokenhearted but not deterred, she committed herself to liberating her parents, family, and friends. She could have been discouraged by those not willing to take the opportunity. She could have been satisfied with saving just her family. They were fugitives in the United States, and so they settled in the bitter cold safety of Ontario, Canada.

> I was the conductor of the Underground Railroad for eight years, and I can say what most conductors can't say; I never ran my train off the track, and I never lost a passenger.
>
> —Harriet Tubman

Once she had freed her family, she knew her job was not completed and kept returning for anyone who could be convinced to leave. She said, "I freed a thousand slaves, I could have freed a thousand more it only they knew they were slaves." When her passengers would threaten to abandon the journey, she had the courage to be willing to kill them rather than risk the life of the other runaways, or the

Underground Railroad agents. She said, "You'll be free or die!" A famous Underground Railroad agent, Thomas Garrett wrote of Harriet Tubman, "Never met with any person, of any color, who had more confidence in the voice of God, as spoken direct to her soul … and her faith in a Supreme Power truly was great." She used that power for liberation. "Slavery," she said, "is the next thing to hell." Fearless, she returned again and again, saying, "I can't die but once." She was willing to give the ultimate sacrifice, her life.

> There are two things I've got a right to, and these are,
> Death or Liberty – one or the other I mean to have.
> No one will take me back alive; I shall fight for my
> liberty, and when the time has come for me to go, the
> Lord will let them, kill me.
>
> —Harriet Tubman

She became an activist. She attended antislavery meeting, black rights conventions, and women's suffrage rallies. She was devoted to equality and justice and was willing to risk her life to release, defend, and protect runaway blacks. As she was involved in the abolitionist movement, Mother Harriet was befriended by John Brown in 1958. He referred to her as "General Tubman," and she helped him plan the surprise attack to liberate enslaved Africans on Harper's Ferry, Virginia, in 1859. Brown was killed in that attack, and Harriet Tubman believed he was a martyr for freedom. That year she moved to Auburn, New York, settling her aging parents and family members surrounded by fervent abolitionists, where the family was supported and protected. She raised money for her family and her mission through antislavery lectures under the pseudonym Harriet Garrison, as she was still actively being pursued by slave catchers. In April of 1860 she helped rescue a fugitive, Charles Nalle, from the custody of the US Marshals trying to return him to Virginia under the fugitive slave act of 1850.

> ...and I prayed to God to make me strong and able to fight, and that's what I've always prayed for ever since.
>
> —Harriet Tubman

She could not rest without becoming a personal warrior and recruiter for the North during the Civil War. Her spiritual guides gave her the trails to follow. The plants talked to her and shared their healing herbs, and she inspired others to join the quest for freedom for all. She became a cook, scout, herbalist, healer, nurse, and spy for the Union Army in South Carolina and cared for newly liberated black soldiers who crowded the Union Camps. Harriet Tubman was the first American woman to lead an armed raid into enemy territory. Mother Harriet's effort in this raid was responsible for liberating over seven hundred enslaved blacks and destroying Confederate outposts and supplies. She witnessed the massacre at Fort Wagner of the all-black Massachusetts Forty-Fifth Regiment and recounted that fateful day: "And then we saw the lightning, and that was the guns; and then we heard the thunder, and that was the big guns; and then we heard the rain falling, and that was the drops of blood falling; and when we came to get in the crops, it was the dead that we reaped." With only 174 Confederate casualties, there were 1,515 black dead or wounded. She cared for hundreds of the injured transported to Beaufort for care. The valor of these black soldiers fighting for their liberation was a turning point for the war and for the Union Army's confidence in the use of black soldiers in the war effort.

> God's time is always near. He set the North Star in the heavens; He gave me the strength in my limbs; He meant I should be free.
>
> —Harriet Tubman

The war ended, and with the ending of slavery, freedom was achieved for all of the slaves. But she realized that the end of slavery was just the beginning of a new journey out of mental slavery and economic deprivation. As a post-war activist, women's suffragette, and Reconstructionist, she continued her work for her people. Despite her own financial trouble, she raised money for the Freedman's Bureau to provide education and relief for millions of newly liberated African people. She was denied back pay for her military services during the civil war. Her humanitarian efforts prevailed with the establishment of the Harriet Tubman Home for the Aged located on land she purchased next to her home. She transferred this institution to the African Methodist Episcopal Zion Church in 1903. She continued to appear at local and national black empowerment meetings and suffrage conventions. She died at the age of ninety at her home in Auburn, New York. Just before she died, Mother Harriet said, "I go to prepare a place for you." She was buried at Fort Hills Cemetery in Auburn, New York, with military honors.

> Read my letter to the old folks, and give my love to them, and tell my brothers to be always watching unto prayer, and when the good old ship of Zion comes along, to be ready to step aboard.
>
> —Harriet Tubman

We all are changing the world whether we realize that or not. Our thoughts are part of the collective unconscious of the universe. The hatred and revenge in my road rage contributes to the war in the world. The bubbles of love I send out to enemies, friends, and anonymous individuals ahead of me caught in a traffic jam leads to the healing, peace, and serenity in the world. The stories of these role models, mentors, friends, and mothers are our stories. They are part of us, and we can propel that positive energy forward. It is our choice where we put our attention and focus. What dreams do we want to manifest in our existence, for our world, and for humanity?

> Every great dream begins with a dreamer. Always remember, you have within you the strength, the patience, and the passion to reach the stars, to change the world.
>
> —Harriet Tubman

In 1944, the National Council of Negro Women sponsored war bonds with the slogan, "Buy a Harriet Tubman war bonds for freedom!" In June of that year, the first liberty ship named for this black woman hero was launched. In 1974 the Harriet Tubman Home for the Aged received National Historic Landmarks Status. In 1978 the US Postal Service issued its first postage stamp in the Black Heritage Series commemorating her legacy. In the 1990s her home was declared a historic landmark as well. The Albany Free School students were studying the life of Harriet Tubman. They uncovered the fact that Harriet Tubman should have received widows' pension from January 1899 to March 1913. They brought it to the attention of Hillary Clinton. In 2003, then Senator Hillary Clinton secured the funding from the widows' pension to maintain Harriet Tubman's home and to honor her memory. Harriet Tubman's estate, however, has yet to receive any compensation for her service as a veteran of the Civil War. There are efforts afoot to secure her image on the US twenty-dollar bill and efforts to block it! Surely our work is far from done.

The annual Race for the Race at my children's school is a fundraiser dedicated to honoring the legacy of Harriet Tubman. For years I was the official physician for the event but later started running the race while going through my tumultuous marriage, separation, and divorce of my fifteen-year marriage. I had two children. I needed to run. I needed freedom. I was running from my life. A wonderful marriage had overnight turned into a nightmare after my husband's estranged mother, herself an alcoholic, had passed. I will never forget that morning after her death, as I tried to console him. He pulled away and scoffed, "Your parents love you. You will never understand!" A wall went up! He became a binge drinker following his mother's footsteps into alcoholism. Year after year, I ran. Six years of emotional turmoil eventually reached a crescendo in what we politely call "the incident," landing me in domestic violence court. I never would have imagined it. I was grateful for my escape, and I needed Godmother Harriet to help me run for my new life.

Spiritual Empowerment

Harriet Tubman is my ancestral Godmother Mother, and I look to her light and life for inspiration in times of whining and complaining. Her spirit carried me through the race training mile after mile. The race was not only to raise money but to raise our hearts and minds and spirits to our victory. Personally, it strengthened me and empowered me spiritually for Al-Anon, the court battle, the custody battle, and almost losing our home. I kept running: running through the turmoil of a rambunctious and rebellious teenager and running through the crisis and transition of a family-run medical office to an independent, solo practice. I kept running through health care transitions, a new marriage, visitation dilemmas, family drama, and my new career as an employed physician. I was fundraising for the financial freedom of the school, but I was running for my freedom.

Harriet Tubman was a woman of her time who took on the challenges of the day: slavery, Civil War, women's suffrage, post-slavery reconstruction, poverty, and care of the elderly and indigent. She was intuitive, a leader, and a natural healer. Her life is inspiration, motivation, action, courage, generosity, healing, perseverance, ingenuity, gratitude, power, grace, and victory. Mother Harriet was dedicated to family, her people, and liberty. She did not just get older; she became an elder. Looking back, she had no regrets, only lessons, and looking forward, she carried no baggage but a legacy of love, sharing, and caring with courage. She followed the call of her heart to escape the terror of slavery. She was in harmony with nature. She was obedient to the guidance of spirit and trusted her intuition to lead her and others. She worked tirelessly for liberty, justice, and equality. It is no wonder I chose this fearless, faithful, and self-determined leader and humanitarian as my Godmother Mother out of respect for a long and productive life well lived.

Our Godmother Mother can help us with our self-doubt, self-sabotage, and self-punishment. She understands that our mistakes are lessons on our road to victory. This mother realizes that all roads lead to glory. She is there for us during our grief and our celebration. She builds our confidence with her love and clarity, bringing us out of self-doubt. She understands our self-punishment through self-sabotage is because of lack of self-esteem, guilt, and regret. With her nonjudgment as our guide, we are able to understand life lessons and use them as stepping stones on our journey up to the mountaintop. She knows we are worthy, and she empowers us to know that too.

Connie Barber

Connie Barber

Constance Roberta Barber was born in Atlanta but raised in Connecticut and would call herself "a Georgia peach with a lot of Connecticut nutmeg." As the middle child, she was rejected by her father for the color of her skin; she was too dark. Although by black standards she would have been considered to have light skin, she would not be considered "light, bright and almost white," which was valued by her family. She was the darkest of her siblings. Her parents were not demonstrative of their love. When she lost her dog, it was a rough time for her. Her dog had been the friend that comforted her. Luckily, as a child she had loving aunties who took her under their wings. She was also very close to her older brother, Buddy. Perhaps these experiences shaped her to be the loving, compassionate, thoughtful, patient, and supportive friend, relative, wife, mother, auntie, grandmother, and godmother to all of us that knew and loved her.

Her mantra: "Read, read, read."

Connie felt reading helped broaden one's perspective. As a child, she developed a passionate love of books and became an insatiable reader. She mothered her younger sister, Juanita, lovingly called Juany, who was ten years her junior, and taught her to read. She was an honor student in high school and college. She loved Howard University. Connie met many lifelong friends there, including her husband of fifty-six years, Jesse Barber. She enjoyed her sister friends, with whom she kept close and to whom she could bear her soul. She was a bookworm and ended up studying library science.

*Next to every **good** man is a **great** woman.*

She supported her husband, Jesse, through his military career and medical training in neurosurgery. They had four children, three boys (Clifton, Jesse, and Charlie) and finally a girl, Joye. Connie had lost her mother when her youngest child, Joye, was just seven years old. Her mother had died alone. Connie started having wild dreams and screaming at night for a period of years. It was a very unsettling time for her. She never remembered those dreams. However, it was a time of spiritual growth, bringing her closer to her Lord. It brought her closer to her siblings as well and instilled in her a love of family. It prompted her desire to take care of her family elders. Over the years, she took in each one of her grandparents and her mother-in-law. When we were in college, Joye became my best friend, and I was taken into the family. She physically took me into their home one summer as a homeless college student.

> Mama loved her children.
>
> —Dr. M. Joye Barber Owens

She was thoughtful and remembered everyone's special occasions; she had a way of making everyone feel special. This is especially true for her children, whom she vowed not to treat coldly as she had been treated by her parents. She was a writer and a poet. She wrote personal letters and poems to her children. The family was never poor; however, she was very frugal. She made sure her children got a good education. She did not give into the fashion fads but bought practical clothing for her children, despite their protests. She never felt the need to keep up with the Joneses. She was thrilled when they paid off their home and this gave her the freedom to be generous to others. She was a faithful donor to many of her heart's causes. She saved their money, and when she passed, left it to her grandchildren.

She was socially conscious and involved with the issues of her time, including desegregation and civil rights. She took in friends from around the country who had come to the historic March on Washington for Jobs and Freedom in 1963. When Martin Luther

King Jr. died, she cried as if a family member had been killed. She was concerned with local as well as the national issues. She shielded her family from a lot of the racism of the time. When they took family vacations in Florida, she packed chicken for the road south so they did not have to stop at segregated locations for food. There were few things to do back then as a family. They drove to a particular area of Florida to swim at a beach that was not segregated. Other times they would stay at someone's house who had a swimming pool. Connie adored swimming and did so as much as she could. I will never forget when she taught me how to do the side stroke. She would glide gracefully through the water as if leading the waves. I still visualize myself as my Godmother Mother Connie Barber, as I gracefully glide through the water swimming the side stroke.

Live and let Live

Connie loved people. Her philosophy went beyond the idea of mere tolerance. She had an acceptance of people's differences. She was a humanitarian. She not only did not judge others but respected all others regardless of the race, sexual orientation, or gender. As a progressive thinker leading the way for our modern day political correctness, this Godmother Mother had an appreciation for people's differences and understood how this diversity made a better world. She knew everyone was worthy. She had a passion to give back to her community. She was a faithful supporter of her church and worked for the food pantry program. She worked with many local groups, medical auxiliaries, and neighborhood organizations. After retiring from years of service as a junior high school librarian, she went back to the elementary schools once a week to read to the children, despite her crippling arthritis. She always made us all feel special.

> Please and thank you, please and thank you, please
> and thank you … manners matter.
>
> —Connie Barber

Connie was passionate about many things. Manners matter. She instilled that into her children at home and into her schoolchildren at work. Connie was a fanatical fan of the Washington football team. Her children were grateful that she never had to choose between food on the table and season tickets. She enjoyed hours of camaraderie playing bridge with her friends. I remember many spontaneous weekend crab feasts at the Barber household enjoying food, family, and friends and having fun.

This Godmother Mother, Connie, who I called Mom Barber, taught me how to receive love and become part of a new family, far from my family. She made me feel like her other little girl. After undergraduate graduation, Mom Barber trusted her daughter Joye, me, and our girlfriend, Janice with her car for a road trip. It took a month to drive from Washington, DC, stopping in various states to visit friends and family, going to our sorority convention Las Vegas, and doing sightseeing along the way. We ended up across the country in California to pick up her son Charlie. We then drove him, his things, and his car in a whirlwind, riding along the southern route back home.

The Peaks and Valleys

I was exhilarated to get a summer research opportunity between my freshman and sophomore years of medical school. I was frustrated when the project extended into my sophomore school year, distracting me from my studies. I was devastated after cramming for my first intersessional tests. My grades plummeted as my mind crashed with my first and last experience ever with NoDoz™. I knew I was in serious academic trouble. I was overjoyed to receive the "More Than a Pair of Hands" award for my summer research project but disappointed not to attend the awards ceremony since I was busy studying at home. I was thrilled when my studying seemed to pay off. My final intersessional grades were my best ever, and I received multiple honors scores. But it was too little too late. I had crashed and burned. I had flunked out of medical school!

I felt so special, loved, and not judged by this loving godmother when this happened. I allowed myself a day of remorse, grief, and self-pity. I was traumatized and overwhelmed, and Mom Barber accepted and supported me with a confidence that helped me pick myself up and get back in the game. I developed a plan. I had gotten into medical school once; I would just have to do it again. I was reassured, respected, and expected to overcome any adversity. I was welcomed and treated with her unconditional love. She exhibited a confidence in me and her children and godchildren, nieces and nephews, grandchildren, and probably students as well, letting us all know that we are worthy.

When I last visited her at home, she was doing well. Her hands were deformed from arthritis, but she reported they were pain free. Connie said she was in need of, and was graciously and gratefully accepting, help from her son Jesse, who had returned home to care for his parents as they developed health problems. It was a tenuous time for life and death. Her husband of over fifty-six years had died less than a year before. I knew the statistics. Many spouses die within a year of their loved one's passing. That was coupled with the tragic death of her nineteen-year-old grandson, Jekonni. He had died in a freak automobile accident shortly before the time of my visit. I wanted to check up on her to see how she was doing. Connie appeared vibrant, vital, and strong, so when I heard shortly thereafter that she had fallen suddenly ill and was in the hospital, I was surprised.

During my visit to see her in the hospital, Connie seemed distant. I thought it was from medications. She was looking upward and asking, "Help me up. Help me up!" I thought she must be uncomfortable in the bed, and I went to adjust her position. She kept repeating, however, "Help me up. Help me up!" I tried and tried to help her, again and again. It was not until later I realized it was not me she was talking to. She had slipped between two worlds and she was asking for help from loved ones on the other side. She had worked out all her demons in her younger life and was ready to go to her *glory*! They helped her up!

This Godmother Mother teaches me to keep myself at peace. We never know when our time will come to make that final transition. I do not wait to forgive myself and others. I do not let my heart become harden with regret, defeat, envy, or bitterness. I choose daily to live a legacy of being. Our legacy of being is how we want to embrace the world! Personally, I choose to live life with enthusiasm, being encouraging and helpful. Our Godmother Mother teaches us about true perfection. Perfection is being our best and doing our best at all times in the effort of wellbeing. We can look back on life with a rearview lens and think things were a mistake. We can look forward with anticipation, and things can then fall short of our expectations. This mother teaches us surrender! With an attitude of nonjudgment, there is the understanding our best is all we can give in that moment. Our best is always good enough! It is perfect. My lesson plan for life is to seek joy, give hope, and feel peace. My mission is to heal and be healed.

I was never as bold as my daughter to demand official paperwork to make this patient, kind, passionate, generous, loving, protective, thoughtful, and wise woman my godmother. But in my heart of hearts, she had this role in my life. A godmother is a spiritual guide for our life lessons. Connie's life was her lesson plan for me, not mere words. She was prudent and thrifty and prepared for her transition, establishing an inheritance for her grandchildren. By living a sensible, productive, happy, and helpful life of service, she ensured this legacy of being for her children, grandchildren, extended family, friends, neighbors, and community. The graceful way she would glide across the water doing a side stroke is a metaphor how I want to live a life of peace, beauty, passion, and quiet power. She showed me how I want to die, in the peace of knowing a faith-filled, meaningful, and enlightened life of service.

Chapter 13

Our Cosmic Mother: Gathering our Mothers' Council

We create the storybook of our life. We assign the meaning to the cast of characters, and we can seek characters for our script. We have the power to make decisions to orchestrate our life, or we have the option to remain a victim of our life, reacting with preconditioned responses to events that seem out of our control. Life itself is an education. It has been said that an unexamined life is a life not fully lived. We can fulfill a lifelong quest for knowledge if we use the opportunity of a thoughtful, contemplative life. We answer the call to witness and attest to what we believe in our life choices. What is our life lessons plan? What do we *want* people to say when they talk about us behind our backs? When we pass from this earth, what is our legacy of being that we want stated after we are gone? Our assembly of moms helps us to do just that. What do we want to learn from these mothers? We can decide who our mothers are to be and what these guides need to teach us.

Our biological mothers come to us with their own challenges that can be helpful to us or can hinder us as their children. These can be minor trials or overwhelming obstacles. We have our personal struggles, family traumas, and also social, national, and global dilemmas that can influence the reactions we have and projections we make into our futures. Our mother did the best she could in the circumstances of her life. I use the term *best* that she could in this specific context: Any wounding from our birth mother is a reflection of her own brokenness and never a reflection of the lack of our worthiness. There are women who have been mean and hateful to their children and have brutalized them either physically or emotionally or both. Their reaction to us, their children, was not personal but part of their unconscious conditioned beliefs and behavioral reactions to their life stressors. Is it not time that we stopped the intergenerational transmission of this brokenness and start a path of healing in our own lives, our children's lives, and our children's, children's lives?

When I was a young mother and while going through my divorce, the discipline I gave to my son was undisciplined. With my second "only child," my daughter, born eleven years later, I was in a much different position of spiritual growth and development. It was an active process. Luckily my son and I have been able to heal those wounds. But I did the best I could in my brokenness at that time. I am also aware that there are mothers who are not trying to heal their brokenness. Sometimes we are so caught up in life that we have not been able to gain any wider perspective to even search for healing. Sometimes suffering is all we know, and we cling to the familiarity of the pain. We can pray for them. We can be their light. But we do not have to allow their darkness to keep us in the shadows. Sometimes our mothers have transcended this life, never finding that place of peace. We can find that peace and change the legacy of our family.

Hopefully life had surrounded us with a village to help raise us as children. Once we come of adult age, is our responsibility to stop blaming the situations of our past for the outcomes of our future. Raising ourselves from cradle to grave is a big job! The sooner we can detach and heal from our childhood wounds, the sooner we can move forward to a life of purpose. We can get help. We can gather our esteemed ancestors, elders, and role models for our Mothers' Council.

Our Cosmic Mother is the universal maternal energy from which our Mothers' Council is drawn. When we determine our brokenness, we can establish a relationship with those mothers that have been able to pick up their pieces and move forward. When we designate those qualities we desire to develop within ourselves, we can use the assistance of our mothers to access these assets for ourselves. If we lack passion we can find a Sexy Mama; if we lack courage we can find a Warrior Mother; if we lack joy we can find a Mother Sister; and if we need healing we can find our Dr. Mom and so forth. When we determine our goals for our purpose in life, we can use the inspiration of our mothers to lead us to our calling.

Unity and the Cosmic Mother—Earth Mother to Godmother

The foundation of teaching any subject is a correct understanding of the guiding principles involved. When learning a new activity, we tend to listen carefully and proceed slowly and cautiously, with no expectation of the outcome. We are open to explore what happens. We call this mindfulness practice beginner's mind. I teach this in my yoga classes. We stay focused and present in the moment. However, if we are judgmental of ourselves or others, we look at others and lose sight of our own experience. Even more practiced students' minds can wander off the moment while expecting past performance but find it does not necessarily work that way. Each circumstance is unique. Beginner's mind, without judgment or comparison, just openness to the moment, brings peace.

Unity is a key principle of our Cosmic Mother. Our entire Mothers' Council is working together simultaneously. Earth Mother and Godmother Mother are the pillars of our mothers' council. They form the beginning and the end of this circle of guides. From Earth Mother we are born into this physical life. Godmother Mother guides us to our eternal spiritual life. We are assisted from our birth to our final transition. It is Mother Earth who is our physical life sustenance, and our Godmother Mother guides our spiritual transitions through our life and as our physical body returns to dust. We are indivisibly connected to the totality of Mother Earth physically and all creation spiritually. When we practice the concept of unity, we promote moral, harmonious interrelationships with nature, within ourselves, and with our family, our local community, our nation, and our global village.

Morality from ancient African societies promoted righteousness—righteous behavior, righteous thoughts and righteous character. In ancient Kemet, now modern-day Egypt, the principles of Maat required seven cardinal virtues: balance, harmony, compassion, justice, order, reciprocity, and truth. The living of these principles allows togetherness. We join together for the benefit of all. We feel deeply when discordant actions tear through our hearts, like the Rwandan genocide, the terrorist acts of 9/11, and domestic violence. To live this unity principle, it is not enough *not* to do any harm; it is required that we lovingly become of service to one another. How gratified we feel as we well up in pride from the self-sacrificing hero who risks or loses his or her life for the benefit of a loved one, a stranger, or a whole community. This feeling of unity is hardwired into us, but we have the choice to ignore it or override it.

Most of us do not live at these radical extremes of tragedy and heroism. However, we contribute to these feelings in our day-to-day attitudes and behaviors. Don't our unkind thoughts contribute to negativity in the world? Don't our feelings of revenge contribute to war and violence? Doesn't our prejudice lead to injustice? And likewise, don't we live a shero's journey by standing for righteousness and truth, daily acts of kindness, and paying it forward instead of crawling over others to get ahead? The old saying, "It is better to give a hand up then a hand out" speaks to this philosophy of unity. When we live in unity, our hands are busy. A lot is being accomplished by the team, like the old African proverb states, "If you want to go fast, go alone; if you want to go far, go together."

We learn these principles by role modeling inclusivity. The unity of our parents provides a foundation for the family and models for the children. How parents treat each other and the children's grandparents and elders provides the context for children's interactions. Dysfunction is now the norm in most families, and often we are learning as much what not to do as what to do in our personal lives. Unfortunately, drama has become the entertainment of today, role modeling harshness, selfishness, and self-centeredness with the need to be validated by attention. It does not appear important whether we are a famous or infamous. There appears to be a desire to be noticed at whatsoever cost. What is *not* seen any more is the complementary nature of the feminine and masculine principles that can work together with fairness, for mutual benefit, and with true kindheartedness!

Unfortunately, even some of our leaders who are elected to serve the society are more concerned with selfish aims than the public good. Inherent to our identity as a moral, ethical, and conscious society, our political imperative must reflect our collective consciousness of goodwill and positive intent. When conflict cannot be avoided, swift, enthusiastic, and honorable resolution should be sought with mutual respect, thoughtfulness, and cooperation. Unity assumes human equality and therefore cultivates social equality. We all invest in each other's progress, happiness, and wellbeing.

Revelation of Spirit

The idea of unity understands the similarity between newborns and elders. They both share a closeness to the spirit world. The newborn is coming from spirit and the elders are preparing to leave the physical plane to go to spirit. This speaks to our family and community development over generations. The cycle of life is strengthened by intergenerational transmission. The civilization we take for granted daily was built from the labor of the generations that came before us. What we leave as our legacy of our life on this earth after our death is based on our contribution during our lifetime. What a blessing and privilege! Our life mission is to leave the world a better place than we found it. Our family mission is to empower each other in service to our mission. We move our communities forward. As we live and evolve as spiritual beings, we do not just get older; we become elders. With years of life experience, we are able to turn problems into opportunities for growth and offer solutions to resolve conflict. The esteemed elders should become the stewards of our nations and our planet, responsible for empowering humanity and caring for Mother Earth.

Unfortunately, this holistic cycle of life happens all too rarely in modern society. Our elders are discarded and not appreciated for the benefit they could provide our society. Instead of meaningful roles, they are retired into isolation, left alone with their fading memories. Too often our elders' pride does not allow them to accept the physical assistance of younger people as their physical health declines. These elders are unaware of their own power and do not realize they have the influence to change the life of a young person, which does change the course of the world.

When the society includes all age groups and young people learn respect and appreciation for their elders, it allows them to understand the process of growing older. Hopefully these youngsters develop a plan to live a contemplative life to cultivate the character and qualities of expert practitioners in the game of life. Our esteemed elders transition to become our honored ancestors that we remember through our rituals and traditions. They become our role models and give us inspiration. Our historical memory of our family, community, and national and global ancestors are powerful stories to share and provide us a cultural framework to live our own shero's journey.

Our Cosmic Mother: Manifesting Our Goals

Assembling our Mothers' Council and putting them to work requires forethought. It is intentional and requires us to seek out these women in our personal life and spiritual life through our historic and contemporary mothers that we know of but do not know personally.

Our imagination gives us an idea. That is our spark of the creator. Our Cosmic Mother reminds us to use our mind's eye and the creativity of our Mother Sister and charge it with positive emotional energy of our Sexy Mama to make things happen. Sexy Mama knows that emotions are tools of manifestation. She knows that passion is the inspiration that leads to the accomplishment of much that occurs in the world. We must put forth a correct emotional effort or our plans do not have the power to hold us through to our final goal. They can be easily dissuaded by others' negative comments. Mother Wit challenges us to keep our plans close to our heart until they are ready to be shared and to make the changes inside ourselves to *be* what we are trying to create in the world. But our Sexy Mama gives us the emotional fuel to take intention into action. Lawyer Mother helps us judge our methods as right and righteous while Mentor Mother provides us a vision for the road ahead with her valuable experience. We look to Warrior Mother to assist us with any battles we face, but with the guidance and spiritual intuition of our Queen Mother combined with the practical plan, organization, and structure provided by our Grandmother Mother. When we get weary, we can be refreshed and rejuvenated by our Earth Mother. When we stumble and fall, we can retreat to the security of our Godmother Mother to give us the strength to try again. When we are injured and hurt, we can rest in the healing embrace of our Dr. Mom. Then the cycle repeats itself. Progress is made. After completing our earthly tasks, with our legacy assured, our Cosmic Mother will be there calling us home.

My Mother's Love

By Deborah L. Bernal, MD

Warm like the summer sunshine,
Soft like an autumn breeze,
My mother's love surrounds me.
I feel her presence constantly,
Though she is far away from me.

She is with me here and now,
Shielded by the safety of her womb,
Nurtured by her life-giving essence.
My mother's love enfolds me.
I am cradled in her comfort.
Though she is far away from me,
She is with me here and now.
Emboldened by my mother's hugs,
Encouraged by her many kisses,
My mother's love embraces me.
I am empowered by her confidence.
Though she is far away from me,
She is with me here and now.
Mentored by the words she talks,
Modeled by the road she walks,
My mother's love guides me.
I am inspired by her life.
Though she is far away from me,
She is with me here and now.

Epilogue

I THANK THE CREATOR FOR the opportunity of this life. I have so much more work to do. I want to thank all these mothers in this circle, my Mothers' Council, for this journey of writing this book. Thank you for the counsel I received from bringing them in my life both virtually and physically. It has truly been a healing experience for me. I have been charged with much more work from this writing. I am grateful to all my patients who inspired me to write this book and my coworkers, friends, and family who provide me with a mirror to look at myself in my actions and reactions. As always, I think I am doing things for somebody else, and again it ends up I am doing it for myself. I am not just my brother and my sister's keeper; I am my brother and my sister. I guess that is how I live out my assignment. Heal and be healed!

At this season of my life, I am entering the fall. It is harvest time. I have gathered much soul wisdom, but I realize I am not at the pinnacle of my development. I have lived long enough, however, to look back and gather the fruits of my labor to share with others. This book is my attempt at canning in a digestible form the sweetness, power, and nutrition to fuel the next season of my life and finally develop a legacy to pass on. I write to share in bite-size portions the goodness and richness that has allowed me to live my absolutely fabulous life. I am so blessed and so grateful, so passionate and purposeful. "My cup runs over" (Psalm 23:5 MEV), so I have plenty more to share.

Printed in the United States
By Bookmasters

Printed in the United States
By Bookmasters